The Ghirardelli Chocolate Cookbook

The Ghirardelli Chocolate Cookbook

Text by Neva Beach

Ten Speed Press

OVER 140 YEARS OF CHOCOLATE MAKING EXPERIENCE

Ten Speed Press
P.O. Box 7123
Berkeley, California 94707
www.tenspeed.com

*Cover and book design by Fifth Street Design,
Berkeley, California*

Photostyling by Fifth Street Design

*Food photography by Bill Schwob,
Emeryville, California*

*All drinks and desserts appearing in photographs
prepared, plated, and styled by pastry chef
Jamie Martin, San Francisco, California.*

*Thanks to Lisa Buckel for her help in finding
just the right props.*

*Distributed in Australia by Simon and Schuster Australia,
in Canada by Ten Speed Press Canada, in New Zealand by
Southern Publishers Group, in South Africa by Real Books,
in Southeast Asia by Berkeley Books, and in the United Kingdom
and Europe by Airlift Book Company.*

*Illustration on page 24 reprinted courtesy of
the Bancroft Library, University of California, Berkeley.*

Library of Congress Cataloging-in-Publication Data

The Ghirardelli chocolate cookbook.
p.cm.
    Includes index.

1.Cookery (Chocolate) 2.Chocolate.
3.Ghirardelli Chocolate Company.
TX767.C5G541995
641.6'374—dc2095-16335   CIP

Printed in Korea

6   7   8   9   10 – 04   03   02   01   00

Contents

Cookies and Bars, *65*

Breads and Pastries, *91*

Confections and Other Desserts, *105*

Sauces and Toppings, *127*

Index, *133*

As sweet as the music
of children's laughter,
as pure as the heart of
a little child . . .

— **Domingo Ghirardelli**

Introduction

GHIRARDELLI'S *Ground Chocolate*

—*your grocer has it*

More than any other food, chocolate delights and enchants, evoking the memories and emotions that nourish our immeasurable passion for it. Aficionados know that there is no such thing as too much chocolate. Some savor their chocolate in solitude, lingering over each bite; others flock to chocolate tastings in blissful submission to their cherished obsession. Chocolate promises and chocolate fulfills. Chocolate tantalizes, and it comforts. Chocolate has soothed fretful children and welcomed tired travelers; mountain climbers have saved their last piece of chocolate to celebrate reaching new heights; suitors have given chocolate to show the depth of their devotion. Chocolate has been used as a stimulant, an aphrodisiac, and a form of currency. And long ago, chocolate played a part in the California Gold Rush of 1849, and in the establishment of one of the world's premier confectioneries—San Francisco's Ghirardelli Chocolate Company.

The Story of Chocolate

This most delectable food begins, strangely enough, as small, bitter purple beans in the pods of the cacao tree. The beans don't look appetizing in their raw state, but, fortunately for us all, three or four thousand years ago someone in South or Central America discovered that a flavor unlike any other was locked inside them. Perhaps he or she plucked a cacao pod to eat the sweet pulp that surrounds the seeds inside, then tossed the seeds into the embers of the cooking fire. The roasting seeds undoubtedly gave off a rich scent, inspiring the discoverer to rake the beans from the coals and put a handful of them on a *metate* (the large stone mortar used for grinding corn). The roasted beans probably cracked easily, and quickly became a buttery paste that the discoverer recognized as something special.

We can't know for sure how chocolate was discovered by the people who enjoyed it first, but we do know that the first cocoa beans to reach Europe were brought back from South America in 1502 by Christopher Columbus. The bags of dried brown beans aroused little interest at the time. Fortunately, the Spanish explorer, Hernando Cortés, brought back more cocoa beans twelve years later. Cortés had been given a drink called *chocolatl* ("bitterwater"), by Aztec Emperor Montezuma, a pungent brew of ground cocoa beans, hot peppers, and vanilla beans. Aztecs believed that the drink offered universal wisdom, godlike energy, and, some say, enhanced sexual powers. Only nobles were allowed to drink *chocolatl*, which was consumed out of golden goblets made exclusively for the purpose. (It is no surprise, then, to learn that the scientific name for chocolate is *theobroma cacoa*, or "god food.")

In the early years of the sixteenth century, an inventive cook in the kitchen of Spain's Queen Isabella I added sugar instead of hot peppers, creating a delicious brew made of roasted, crushed cocoa beans whipped up with hot water or milk, sweetened with sugar or honey, and flavored with vanilla, cinnamon, or other spices. The Spanish aristocracy was quickly swept by the new rage.

Initially, scarcity may have had something to do with the beverage's exclusive appeal at first. The cacao tree will only grow within 20 degrees of the equator, and every bean had to be brought to Europe by ship in a journey that took months or, sometimes, years. Overwhelming demand, combined with limited supply, resulted in ever-higher prices for the scarce cocoa beans, and led to increased status for those who could afford them. Consequently, exquisite porcelain pots and cups specially made for serving the beverage were displayed in every affluent home. Meanwhile, the canny Spanish were using chocolate to help build their empire by introducing the cacao tree in each new equatorial land they colonized. Some, however, had their doubts about chocolate. Joseph Acosta, a Jesuit missionary in South America, for instance, noted his skepticism in the late 1500s:

> *The chief use of this Cocoa is a drincke which they call Chocolate, whereof they make great account, foolishly and without reason; for it is loathsome to such as are not acquainted with it, having a skumme or froth that is very unpleasant to taste...Yet it is a drincke very much esteemed by the Indians, whereof they feast noble men as they pass through their country.*

The supply of cocoa beans slowly increased, and the price eventually dropped enough for them to be available to more people. First in Europe, then across the English channel, "chocolate houses"—clubbish places where men of affairs gathered to talk and drink hot chocolate—sprang up throughout the towns and villages. Eventually, the chocolate craze returned to the continent from which it had come. Only this time, the passion for chocolate spread to the northern part, to colonial America.

The first cocoa beans in North America reached Dorchester, Massachusetts, in 1765 and it wasn't long before the colonies also had their own flourishing chocolate houses. Thomas Jefferson was twenty-two years old when chocolate arrived in the colonies. He promptly declared it superior to coffee or tea for health and nourishment, and, thus, it is not unlikely that early drafts of the *Declaration of Independence* were debated and refined over cups of hot chocolate in Williamsburg and Philadelphia.

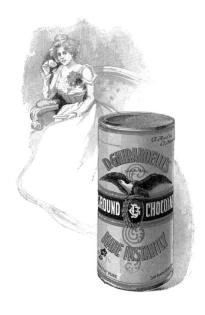

The Apprentice from Italy

In Italy, another chapter in the story of chocolate was just beginning. By the time Thomas Jefferson died in 1826, America had been a nation for thirty-seven years and Domingo Ghirardelli of Rapallo, Italy, was eleven years old. By then, he had already learned a great deal about chocolate while working as an apprentice to a Genoa candymaker. He was also more worldly than most young Italians. Domingo's father was an importer of exotic foods and spices, and in the Ghirardelli home, the names of far-off places, such as Ceylon, Sumatra, and Peru, were part of daily conversation. From an early age, the boy must have known that the world was full of exciting opportunities for those with the imagination and courage to seek them out. Domingo had both, as well as ambition, keen intelligence, and a craft that was likely to be useful no matter where he went. Driven by his adventurous spirit, Domingo Ghirardelli, just nineteen years old and newly married, sailed off to South America.

Domingo first went to Uruguay, where he worked in a coffee and chocolate establishment. After a year, still seeking the right place to settle, he and his wife moved to Lima, Peru, where rumor held that the opportunities for ambitious young men were greater. Sadly, Domingo's wife died soon after they arrived. In time he remarried, taking the hand of Carmen Alvarado, a widow with a baby daughter.

In Lima, one of the happiest coincidences in chocolate history occurred when the Ghirardellis moved into a small building on Mercadero Street, next door to an enterprising U.S. cabinetmaker and piano builder named James Lick. The two young businessmen had much in common. Both were ambitious and intelligent, and both were fascinated by the news of discoveries and opportunities in North America. Finally, Lick decided he had to go see for himself. As his destination, he chose a place in California Territory called Yerba Buena, or, by those who had the latest information, San Francisco. Lick was a bachelor, free to pick up and go where he liked. Domingo stayed behind in Peru, probably because he had a wife and a family, but, as a way of joining in Lick's adventure vicariously, he sent six hundred pounds of chocolate in his friend's baggage.

James Lick landed in San Francisco on January 11, 1848. Just thirteen days later, gold was discovered at Sutter's Mill. But even before that historic day, Lick had written back to Ghirardelli in Peru, saying:

> *This is a place of opportunity, and I would suggest that you bring yourself and some of your chocolates up here. I have sold the 600 pounds that I brought and I feel there will be a great demand for it.*

Ghirardelli wasted no time. Making sure his wife and children were comfortably established in Lima, he took his friend's advice and left for California, sailing into San Francisco Bay aboard the Peruvian *Mazeppa* on February 24, 1849. Four days later, the steamship *California* brought the first boatload of fortune-hunting prospectors.

Purveyor of Sundries and Chocolate

Like most newcomers in those heady times, Domingo did his stint in the gold fields, but soon realized he wasn't a miner. He turned to a trade he knew better, opening a store in a tent in Stockton, California, to sell supplies to miners. The store was immediately successful, so he opened another in San Francisco, then built a hotel there as well. On the side, he began grubstaking prospectors in exchange for a share of any gold they might find. His next venture was a "French Soda Fountain," also opened in Stockton.

Although he certainly wouldn't be the only man to make a fortune in the California Gold Rush, he was one of the first, and one of the very few to build a company that endures to this day. Ghirardelli shrewdly saw that the exhausted miners in from the fields would be starved for luxuries, and that the lucky ones would need something to spend their gold dust on. He stocked primarily delicacies: coffee, dried fruits, spices, and, as one of his early advertisements boasted, "Foreign cognacs, Wines and Liquours, Native Wines, English, French, Japan, and East India goods." And he carried, of course, the most popular delicacies of all—chocolate, and chocolate candies, some imported and some manufactured in his own shop.

San Francisco was growing rapidly, doubling and tripling its population again and again as men from all over the world came in search of gold. After a while, women and children began arriving too, bringing a domesticating influence to the rough and raucous boomtowns of the area—and a new market for Ghirardelli's treats. Housing was scarce. Most people had to be content with shacks or tents that could be thrown up in a hurry, made from whatever materials were at hand. Often, in this timber-rich land, it was hastily milled fir and redwood that was available for building. Heating was provided by wood fires, and lighting came from candles and oil lanterns. It should be no shock, then, that the vulnerable young cities were swept by fire time and again. On May 3, 1851, the fifth in a series of San Francisco fires destroyed an estimated 1,500 buildings, including Ghirardelli's store and hotel. Three days later, another fire consumed half of Stockton. In less than a week, all of Ghirardelli's businesses were wiped out.

Domingo Ghirardelli was not devastated by disaster. He not only recovered from his losses, but within a year he'd opened a coffeehouse and formed a new confectionery company. In 1852, he relocated the thriving business to a bigger building at the corner of Washington and Kearney streets in San Francisco, the first home of what was to become the Ghirardelli Chocolate Company. With his businesses well established, Domingo brought his family from Peru to their new home in San Francisco. There were three children; in time, the first American generation of Ghirardellis would number seven.

Refining the Art of Chocolate Making

As chocolate became more popular, some of the early methods of making chocolate were found lacking. By 1660 or so, the first generation of chocolate candy had been made in Europe of roasted and ground cocoa beans combined with sugar and pressed into cakes. However, the confection was fairly coarse and gritty. Even the popular hot chocolate drink that introduced Europeans to chocolate was tempermental and difficult to make properly from the powdered whole cocoa beans that were its base. Cocoa beans are very rich; more than half their weight is cocoa butter, and as a result it was hard to get the ground whole beans to combine well with liquids. Combining them with hot milk worked tolerably well because of the unusually low melting point of the cocoa butter—about 89 to 93 degrees. Special whisks were used to whip the drink to a smooth consistency and to prevent the cocoa butter and liquid from separating as they cooled in the cup.

A discovery at Ghirardelli factory heralded a revolution in the way chocolate was made and consumed in America. One afternoon in 1865, a Ghirardelli worker put a batch of ground cocoa beans in a cloth bag and hung the bag from a hook overnight. By morning, a pool of cocoa butter had collected on the floor. The ground chocolate left in the bag was almost free of fat—creating a dryer powder that combined with liquids much more smoothly. This became the basis for Ghirardelli's popular Sweet Ground Chocolate and Cocoa. People loved the richness and ease of preparing it and sales flourished. The dripping bags were soon replaced by presses previously invented by an Amsterdam chocolatier, Conrad van Houten, which accomplished the same result in a more controlled way. With popular new products and improved processing, the Ghirardelli company prospered. Three of Domingo's seven children came into the business, furnishing enough Ghirardellis to handle the expansion of business in the United States and abroad.

A Time of Uncertainty and Change

It seemed as if nothing could threaten the thriving company's growth. But no company can ever be entirely safe. When a depression hit the nation in the late nineteenth century, the Ghirardelli Chocolate Company, with its diversified holdings and investments, proved to be vulnerable after all. In 1870 Ghirardelli was forced into bankruptcy; even the family home had to be auctioned.

Once again Domingo pulled success from the midst of disaster. He not only rebuilt his company, he scrupulously paid off every penny of debt and emerged with better credit than ever. A revolution in transportation helped speed the recovery. Before the first transcontinental railway, products made in California, such as Ghirardelli chocolates, could only reach eastern U.S. markets by ship. But rail transportation took over in 1867, and in three short years the ship tonnage out of San Francisco dropped by almost half. Faster, cheaper rail transportation gave Ghirardelli access to vast new markets of chocolate lovers in the East.

Rail transport was just one of the significant advances in the chocolate business. More people could be reached, but new kinds of chocolate were also being developed to offer them. A Swiss chocolatier, Daniel Peter, found a way to add milk to unsweetened chocolate to deliver a milder, creamier chocolate. Suddenly the palette of chocolate flavors and variety of chocolate products increased dramatically. Americans loved the new milk chocolate and Ghirardelli chocolate masters were soon formulating the company's own milk chocolate blends and developing new confectionary to satisfy the demand.

The Ghirardelli Chocolate Company's focus was changing. The company had done some business in coffee and spices, including mustard grinding for Domingo's friend August Schilling. But by the time Domingo Ghirardelli retired as head of the company in 1892, chocolate had become the dominant product. When his oldest son, Domingo Jr., became president, the business was thriving and healthy. Domingo Jr. was as well matched with the time and place as his father had been a generation earlier. Under his direction, the Ghirardelli Chocolate Company was launched on another period of extraordinary innovation and success. This time, however, the company adopted an artistic flair, as its new president became one of the first U.S. manufacturers to fully understand and use the power of advertising and promotion. He hired the best available artists and advertising experts to saturate the West with the Ghirardelli name and logo to sell Ghirardelli's expanding line of chocolate products. The company perfected its famous Sweet Ground Chocolate and Cocoa, and successfully promoted it to a nation of homemakers as a quick and easy way to make a nourishing milk drink. Because it needed no melting, the ground chocolate was also a handy way to make chocolate cakes, cookies, and candies. Richer and smoother than cocoa alone, Ghirardelli's Sweet Ground Chocolate and Cocoa soon became a household staple and remains to this day the company's flagship product. More elaborate new products were introduced as improvements in manufacturing made it easier to form chocolate and combine it with other ingredients such as nuts, fruits, and flavorings.

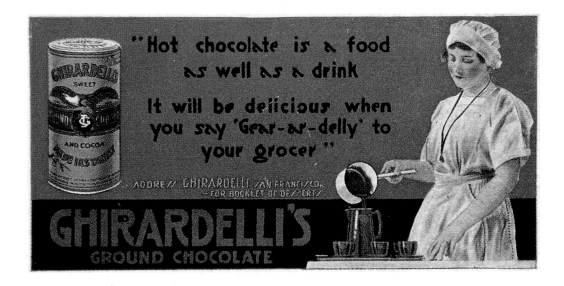

The Making of Ghirardelli Square

With chocolate making growing ever more complex, the company needed a larger site. In 1893 Ghirardelli bought the Woolen Mill Building, a large brick structure facing North Point Street in San Francisco's waterfront district. It was a fortunate choice; when the earthquake struck in 1906, it scarcely rattled the sturdy building. New buildings were added as the company continued to grow; first there was the Mustard Works and Chocolate Building in 1911, a few years later, the Power House, and then an office building and employee apartment house. The complex was completed when the Clock Tower was built on the corner of North Point and Larkin streets.

Beautifully designed in the style of the French Château Blois, the Clock Tower presided grandly over an entire block of Ghirardelli buildings. Executive offices occupied its top floors; beneath were stables for the dray horses that hauled sacks of cocoa beans from the piers at the Embarcadero and carried chocolate products back to the ships and railyards for shipment to Ghirardelli's ever-widening world market. In this one block, the company performed its elaborate chocolate-manufacturing operations and generated its own power (some of it by burning cocoa bean hulls), furnished housing to some of its employees, and even made its own cans and shipping crates.

Ghirardelli was quick to add chocolate bars to its line when new chocolate-molding technology was developed. Once premium chocolate was available in this conveniently portable form, the nation's love of chocolate transformed into a passion. Ghirardelli obliged its public by designing bars with nuts, fruit, and other variations, depending on the tastes of the times. World War I found the company well-equipped to handle the challenge of supplying millions of chocolate bars to U.S. armed forces in Europe.

The Ghirardelli Chocolate Company's block of beautiful buildings was not only a model of self-contained industry, it was fast becoming one of San Francisco's best-known landmarks. The finishing touches were added in 1923, when extra stories were built onto the Cocoa Building and, in a burst of justified pride, the 15-foot-high, illuminated Ghirardelli sign was erected atop the line of buildings on North Point. The sign was so prominent on the San Francisco waterfront that visitors arriving by sea could read it as they passed under the Golden Gate Bridge.

In 1942 the company's giant sign was darkened by World War II blackouts, and Ghirardelli chocolate bars went to war for the second time. After the war, the sign was relighted, but the company itself seemed tired, without the energy and creativity that had characterized it for so long. Stagnation was becoming a greater threat than financial disaster, wars, or epidemics. The family was torn over the company's future; one member even proposed tearing down the historic buildings and replacing them with a block of apartments. People all over the city were alarmed. San Francisco without Ghirardelli was unthinkable.

In the early 1960s, two members of another prominent San Francisco family came to the rescue. William Matson Roth and his mother, Mrs. William P. Roth, proposed a bold new concept: a modern specialty shopping center that would both preserve the historic block of buildings where the Ghirardelli factory was located and provide funds needed to restore and maintain them. They bought the Ghirardelli property and commissioned the architectural firm of Wurster, Bernadi & Emmons to renovate the building in a way that would preserve the Victorian flavor of the block. Only one building, the one that housed a wooden box factory, had to be removed; another was designed to take its place, called the Wurster Building in tribute to the square's chief architect.

The buildings and land were secured, but still no solution to the chocolate company's other problems had been found. Then, in 1963, another Bay Area food company, Golden Grain, bought the factory. Determined to bring the company back to its prominence in American chocolate-making, they moved the Ghirardelli operations to their big, modern Golden Grain plant across the bay. The seemingly impossible had happened. Both the chocolate company and its landmark home were saved.

San Francisco declared Ghirardelli Square an official city landmark in 1965. By 1969 all of its buildings were open, offering an impressive total of 176,000 square feet of some of the city's most desirable retail space. Ghirardelli Square, a model for the restoration of classic buildings, has since also been granted National Historic Register status. In the Ghirardelli Chocolate Manufactory, a soda-fountain where ice cream and Ghirardelli chocolate is sold, exhibits show visitors how it all began nearly a century and a half ago. From its modern factory across the bay, the Ghirardelli Chocolate Company continues to improve its methods of chocolate making and to develop new flavors and combinations of chocolate confections and baking ingredients.

From Bean to Baking Bar

To make airy chocolate dessert soufflés, aromatic cakes, and butter-smooth fudge, it is crucial to select cooking chocolates that respond to mixing, melting, and baking, and that combine with other foods in a consistent, predictable way. Making chocolate of this quality demands both art and science at every step.

Choosing just the right blend of raw cocoa beans is the first challenge. Chocolate comes not from just one kind of cocoa bean, but from several, each with its own distinctive flavor. *Forastero*, the basic staple bean, makes up 90 percent of the world's crop; exotic varieties such as *Criollo* and *Arriba* are used to add subtle highlights and tones to the base flavor. It takes knowledgeable and artful blenders to find the combination that's just right for a specific form of chocolate. A good robust blend for baking chocolate, for example, might include beans from Ghana, the Ivory Coast, and South and Central America, while a milk chocolate blend would include milder flavored beans from Java, Samoa, and Africa. Domingo Ghirardelli's West Coast location was most easily supplied with South and Central American beans, which lent his chocolate a distinctly richer, more pronounced chocolate flavor than chocolates made from African beans.

To complicate the chocolate-maker's task still further, each cocoa bean variety is harvested, fermented, and dried under varying local conditions. All of these variables cause subtle differences in the flavor of the beans, as do weather conditions, and local fermenting and drying operations. At Ghirardelli, each batch of cocoa beans is carefully sampled, tested, and tasted when it arrives to be certain it meets the standards required for the master-product formulas. Only four people in the company are authorized to evaluate the beans. Any beans that don't measure up are sold to other companies that make nonfood products.

The ultimate flavor and texture of the chocolate also depends on how artfully and carefully the beans are processed. For example, cocoa beans arrive from the fields with thin, papery hulls. Most manufacturers leave the hulls on while the beans are roasted, and remove them later. But chocolate absorbs even the slightest hint of off-flavors, so roasting the hulls can contaminate the blend. To eliminate this risk, in 1982 Ghirardelli was the first U.S. company to adopt a European process which sends beans in shallow trays through a very quick infra-red heating process, vibrating them at the same time to loosen the hulls. The hulls are then easily winnowed off and the beans cracked into coarse bits, or "nibs." Roasting the nibs alone results in a fuller roasted, deeper flavor.

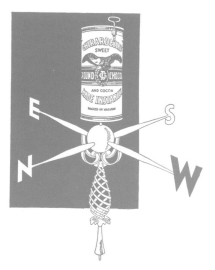

Roasting introduces yet another set of variables. The chocolate-makers must decide, based on experience and their mastery of the craft, just how long and how hot to roast the nibs to bring out precisely the flavor desired. At Ghirardelli, many batches of nibs are also "dutched" first—put through a solution of potassium carbonate—to neutralize acids and to develop a stronger chocolate flavor and a darker color. Then the beans are ground, or milled, until they emerge, at last, as chocolate "liquor"—the essence of pure chocolate.

By the end of the process, 100 pounds of cocoa beans have become about 12 pounds of shell, 8 pounds of water, and about 80 pounds of pure, unsweetened liquor. At this point, the chocolate-making process splits into two tracks. Some of the liquor is pressed to make cocoa butter and cocoa powder, while the rest is blended to make pure chocolate. A portion of liquor is combined with ingredients such as milk or sugar, and may go through several more steps including another grinding, refining through rollers, or warming in a hot water bath to make the different types of chocolate.

The bitter beans of the cacao tree are now almost at the end of the their long transformation. In one final step, the chocolate is "conched"—swept by rotating sets of paddles in giant vats, back and forth, for up to fourteen hours. This carefully timed smoothing process puts the finishing touch on the chocolate. Conching reduces moisture, drives off any lingering acidic flavors, and coats each particle of chocolate with a layer of cocoa butter. Too much conching will make the chocolate excessively oily; too little will leave the flavor undeveloped. But when the ideal level is achieved, the result is a smooth chocolate that has made Ghirardelli Chocolate Company a leading producer of fine chocolate in the United States.

And Now to the Kitchen

Visions of chocolate nourish the soul, but sooner or later the hunger for real fulfillment demands action. Browse through the recipes that follow, pondering chocolate's infinite possibilities. What would complement the day, the mood, the occasion? Perhaps it will be a classic dish with a new twist, such as the Baked Alaska with Zabaglione Sauce, or the absurdly simple but inspired Chocolate–De Menthe Sauce spooned over a dish of vanilla bean ice cream. Maybe the enticement will come in the form of the Devil's Food Cake with Mocha Buttercream Frosting, or the intriguing combinations of flavors in Chocolate Hazelnut-Pear Tart.

Before you select a recipe to prepare, we recommend that you read the following chapter, where you'll find useful information about cooking with our chocolate, including how to melt it correctly, how to store it, and much more. You'll also find instructions for creating simple garnishes that will add a classic touch to your baked goods, a list of ingredients called for in the recipes and what, if anything, may be substituted for certain ingredients. Lastly, you'll find an annotated list of our chocolate baking products, which are produced to ensure that your efforts will be rewarded with a masterpiece every time you cook with Ghirardelli chocolate. We hope you enjoy these recipes and will continue to make Ghirardelli chocolate an essential ingredient in the good food and great memories you share with friends and family.

About the Recipes and Cooking with Ghirardelli Chocolate

The Types of Chocolate

Successful chocolate dishes depend first and foremost on the chocolate used. Quality is critical. Cooking chocolates must respond to mixing, melting, and baking and must combine with other foods in a consistent, predictable way. Ghirardelli chocolates have been formulated and refined over nearly a century and a half to meet these requisite high standards.

Each recipe in this book calls for specific Ghirardelli chocolate products, with the right texture, flavor, and cooking characteristics needed for the dish being prepared. While it may be possible to substitute other forms of chocolate in some recipes, the best results come from using the chocolate product called for in each recipe. Keep a variety of chocolates on hand, so you'll be ready when inspiration strikes.

Here is a list of the Ghirardelli products used in this cookbook, and instructions for the proper storage.

Unsweetened Chocolate Baking Bar: Pure unsweetened chocolate. Used for cooking and baking.

Bittersweet Chocolate Baking Bar: Very dark chocolate containing 55 percent unsweetened chocolate, a small amount of sugar, and vanilla.

Semi-Sweet Chocolate Baking Bar and Semi-Sweet Chocolate Chips: A combination of cocoa butter, sugar, chocolate liquor, and vanilla. Made with 45 percent unsweetened chocolate.

Sweet Dark Chocolate Baking Bar: A combination of chocolate liquor, sugar, vanilla, and cocoa butter. Contains 35 percent unsweetened chocolate.

Milk Chocolate Bar and Milk Chocolate Chips: A blend of chocolate liquor, cocoa butter, sugar, vanilla, and milk powder. The most favored chocolate for eating, also used in cooking and baking.

Sweet Ground Chocolate and Cocoa: An exclusive Ghirardelli product, containing unsweetened chocolate, cocoa, sugar, and vanilla. Used for baking and in milk for hot chocolate drinks.

Premium Unsweetened Cocoa: Pure chocolate powder, made by removing most of the cocoa butter from the chocolate liquor during processing. Ghirardelli cocoa contains 22 to 24 percent cocoa butter. This is a natural process (non-Dutched) cocoa. Used for baking and hot drinks.

Classic White Confection Baking Bar and Classic White Chips: Contains cocoa butter, sugar, and vanilla. The cocoa butter retains a subtle chocolate flavoring, which gives these products their distinctive taste.

Storing Chocolate

All chocolate products should be wrapped tightly when storing to protect them from odors and moisture. Odors are the greatest threat, since chocolate absorbs odors readily and there is no way to remove them. Moisture and heat can cause chocolate to develop a greyish coating called "bloom," but this doesn't affect flavor or interior color.

Chocolate should be kept in a cool cupboard or pantry at a temperature between 60° and 70°F and at a relative humidity of less than 50 percent. The flavor of dark chocolate can actually improve with aging, growing deeper and mellower. These products can be stored for up to two years under the right conditions.

Milk chocolate can be stored for up to one year under the right conditions (as described above).

Pure Unsweetened Premium Cocoa and Sweet Ground Chocolate and Cocoa are slightly less sensitive to storage conditions, but should be kept tightly covered in a cool, dry place. They will be fresh for up to two years.

Chocolate's Nutritional Value

Contrary to popular belief, chocolate is not full of "empty calories." A 1½-ounce bar of milk chocolate, for example, contains about 4 percent of the recommended daily allowance (RDA) of protein, almost 9 percent of the RDA of riboflavin, more than 7 percent of the RDA for calcium, and more than 3 percent of the RDA for iron. Chocolate does contain caffeine, but 1 ounce of milk chocolate has just 6 milligrams of caffeine compared to the average 60 to 120 milligrams found in a cup of coffee.

It is true that cocoa butter has a high level of saturated fat. However, cocoa butter is also high in stearic acids, which recent research indicates may be helpful in reducing cholesterol levels in the blood.

It certainly can't be said that chocolate is a health food. People on sugar- or sodium-free diets should be careful about their chocolate intake. But it is safe to say that chocolate is not worse for us than many other common foods, and more delicious than most.

Ingredients and Substitutions

The recipes in this book use salted butter, all-purpose flour, whole milk, and large eggs. Substitutions may be made in some recipes, but for the most reliable results, use the ingredients listed.

Cooks who enjoy experimenting might want to try some of these alternative ingredients, which also combine well with chocolate:

Nuts

When nuts are used primarily for texture or garnish, these substitutions usually work well: Walnuts or hazelnuts may be substituted for almonds. Pecans and walnuts may be used interchangeably. Almonds may be used in place of hazelnuts.

Liqueurs

Many recipes call for liqueurs. If the liqueur is the main flavoring in a dish, substitution will significantly change its taste. If that is acceptable, then almost any fruit-, nut-, or coffee-flavored liqueur can be used in place of another. Plain brandy can sometimes be successfully used in place of flavored liqueurs, but the flavor will not be as rich.

Chocolate

Ghirardelli Bittersweet and Semi-Sweet Chocolate may be used interchangeably.

Ghirardelli Unsweetened Chocolate and Ghirardelli Chocolate Semi-Sweet baking bars: 4 ounces Ghirardelli Semi-Sweet Chocolate equals 2 ounces Ghirardelli Unsweetened Chocolate combined with 2 ounces sugar.

Ghirardelli Unsweetened Premium Cocoa and Ghirardelli Sweet Ground Chocolate and Cocoa: For each ½ cup unsweetened premium Cocoa, use 1 cup of Sweet Ground Chocolate and Cocoa and decrease the amount of sugar the recipe calls for by ½ cup.

Ghirardelli Unsweetened Chocolate and Unsweetened Premium Cocoa: For every 1 ounce of Unsweetened Chocolate called for in a recipe, use 3 level tablespoons of Unsweetened Premium Cocoa and 1 extra tablespoon of butter, margarine, or vegetable shortening, as called for in the recipe.

Ghirardelli Sweet Ground Chocolate and Cocoa and Ghirardelli Unsweetened Baking Chocolate: For every 1 ounce of Ghirardelli Unsweetened Baking Chocolate, use 6 level tablespoons of Sweet Ground Chocolate and Cocoa; add 1 extra tablespoon of butter, margarine, or vegetable shortening, as called for in the recipe; and decrease the amount of sugar the recipe calls for by 3 level tablespoons.

cakes desserts icings

everything you make with

Chocolate

tastes better when you use

Ghirardelli's

the original GROUND CHOCOLATE

Melting Chocolate

Chocolate will melt faster when broken in small pieces. A sharp knife may be carefully used for cutting baking bars, or use your fingers to break the bars into pieces. Refrigerating chocolate for ½ hour will make it easier to break. Several general rules apply to melting chocolate:

1. Chocolate melts easily at very low temperatures. Use low heat. Heat that's just a few degrees too high can make the chocolate "seize"—become stiff or grainy.

2. Do not let any liquid touch the chocolate. Just a few drops of water can cause the chocolate to become stiff or grainy. Be sure all utensils and containers that might come into contact with the melting chocolate are thoroughly dry before using them.

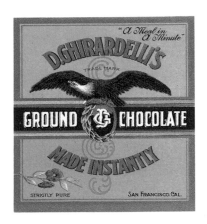

Indirect heat: Using indirect heat guarantees the best results. If you don't have a double boiler use a saucepan and a heat-proof bowl that is slightly wider than the top of the saucepan. Fill the saucepan with enough water to just touch the bottom of the upper container. Use a double boiler, or heat the water to just below boiling. Remove the saucepan from the heat and place the chocolate chunks in the upper container. Allow to sit, stirring every minute or so, for 5 to 10 minutes, or until melted. If any lumps remain, stir the chocolate until it is smooth.

Direct heat: This is by far the riskiest method, but a few expert cooks swear by it. Put the chocolate in a heavy saucepan over the lowest possible heat, and stir continuously until melted.

Microwave oven: Microwaves vary greatly in intensity and evenness of heat, so you may have to experiment to find the best setting. Try a medium setting, allowing 1 to 2 minutes for 1 ounce of chocolate; add 10 seconds for each additional ounce. Chocolate retains its shape when melted in a microwave, so you will need to stir it to test for doneness. If lumps remain, heat again on medium in 15-second increments, stirring after each increment, until thoroughly melted.

Decorating with Chocolate

Chocolate can be as delicious to look at as it is to eat. Dark brown chocolate curls transform a plain pudding into an extravagant treat. A chocolate mousse wreathed in chocolate leaves is a special finish to an elegant formal dinner.

When preparing chocolate for coating (as for making the Chocolate Bowls), it's important to "temper" it during the melting process. **To temper chocolate**, divide the amount into thirds and melt two thirds in a double boiler just until the chocolate is liquid and smooth (110°to 120°F). When it is smooth, add the remaining third of chocolate. Turn off the heat and stir until it all becomes smooth again. Once the chocolate is smooth, proceed as the instructions direct.

Here are some techniques to add flair to your favorite dessert recipes.

Chocolate Curls and Shavings

To make any of the following curls, use a 4-ounce bar of semi-sweet, bittersweet, or milk chocolate.

For large curls, melt the chocolate in a double boiler (see page 17). Turn a baking sheet upside down. Using a plastic spatula, spread the melted chocolate evenly over the baking sheet. (The chocolate should be the thickness of a butter-knife blade.) Refrigerate 10 minutes, or until the chocolate is firm but not brittle. Hold a metal spatula upside down and press firmly into the chocolate, then push steadily ahead until a curl forms. With a toothpick or a small skewer, carefully lift the curls and place them on the dessert, or store them on a plate in the refrigerator until needed.

For small curls, let the chocolate bar stand in a warm place (80 to 85 degrees) until thoroughly warm but not melted. Using a vegetable peeler, make curls by drawing the peeler along the thin, flat side of the bar. Remove the curls with a toothpick and place them on the dessert, or store them on a plate in the refrigerator until needed.

To make shavings, proceed as directed for small curls but use a short stroke when peeling. For a more splintered effect, use cool rather than warmed chocolate. Both shavings and splinter curls work best when made directly over the dessert being decorated. (Practice first over a plate to be sure it's working properly.)

Chocolate Cutouts

**4 ounces (1 baking bar) Ghirardelli Semi-Sweet
Chocolate**

1 tablespoon light corn syrup

Melt the chocolate in a double boiler (see page 17) or acceptable substitute. Line a 9 x 9-inch baking pan with waxed paper.

Stir the light corn syrup into melted chocolate and pour the mixture into the pan. Chill 15 to 20 minutes, or until firm.

Roll the chocolate mixture between two pieces of plastic wrap to form a sheet the approximate thickness of a butter-knife blade. Chill briefly. Using a cookie cutter or small, sharp knife, cut decorative shapes. Peel off the top layer of plastic and lift any excess chocolate from around the cutouts; set aside to roll again. Carefully lift the shapes with a spatula. Use to decorate a dessert, or serve alone.

Chocolate's Flavor Cocoa's Convenience

1 FORM OF CHOCOLATE
FOR EVERY CHOCOLATE USE

GHIRARDELLI'S
THE ORIGINAL
GROUND CHOCOLATE

Chocolate Leaves

**4 ounces (1 baking bar) Ghirardelli Semi-Sweet or
Bittersweet chocolate**

2 teaspoons vegetable shortening

**15 to 20 leaves from a camellia shrub, citrus tree, ivy, or
other plant with stiff, smooth leaves**

Line a baking sheet with waxed paper. Clean the leaves with cold water and dry thoroughly. In a double boiler, melt the chocolate (see page 17) and shortening. Cool the mixture slightly until thick and cool to the touch. With one hand, hold one leaf by the stem, underside facing up. Support the leaf from below with your fingers. With a small metal or rubber spatula, paint the chocolate thickly on the underside of the leaf. Place on the prepared baking sheet, chocolate side up. Repeat these steps until all chocolate is used.

Cool 10 minutes, or until well set. Paint a second coat of chocolate over the first layer. Chill 1 hour, or until very hard. Carefully peel the leaf off the chocolate and transfer the chocolate leaf to the dessert.

Chocolate-Dipped Pecans

4 ounces (1 baking bar) Ghirardelli Semi-Sweet Chocolate

1 teaspoon vegetable shortening

3 dozen pecan halves

Line a baking sheet with waxed paper.

Melt the chocolate and vegetable shortening in a double boiler (see page 17), stirring occasionally until well blended and thoroughly melted. Remove from the heat. Holding a pecan vertically dip halfway into the chocolate and place flat side down on a prepared baking sheet lined with wax paper. Repeat until all pecans have been dipped.

Transfer the baking sheet to a cool place and allow the chocolate to set, approximately 45 minutes to 1 hour.

Drizzling or Piping Chocolate

To generously drizzle a dessert with chocolate, melt 2 ounces (½ baking bar) Ghirardelli Bittersweet, Semi-Sweet, or Milk Chocolate in a double boiler (see page 17), stirring occasionally until chocolate has melted. Prepare a small parchment pastry bag with a hole the desired drizzle size.

Remove chocolate from the heat and spoon into prepared bag. Squeezing the pastry bag, drizzle dessert with melted chocolate.

Chocolate Bowls

4 ounces (1 baking bar) Ghirardelli Milk Chocolate
6 to 8 small balloons (water balloons work well)

In a double boiler melt and temper the chocolate (see page 17); cool until smooth and slightly thickened. Inflate balloons until they are 4 to 5 inches across at their largest point; knot the stems. Holding one balloon by its stem, lower it 2 inches into the chocolate. Rotate the balloon slightly to be sure the top edges of the bowl will be thickly coated. Holding the balloon by its stem, carefully place it on a baking sheet so the chocolate-coated bottom is level (some chocolate will slide down to form a base for the bowl). When all the balloons are dipped, refrigerate them until thoroughly chilled (approximately 45 minutes).

With a sharp toothpick, carefully prick each balloon just below the knot on its stem. The balloon will collapse slowly, leaving a chocolate bowl. Remove and discard the balloon. Refrigerate the bowls until just before serving. Fill with cooled pudding, ice cream, sorbet, candies, or another dessert.

Drinks

Chocolate-Orange Cooler

YIELD: TWO 16-OUNCE SERVINGS

½ cup orange juice concentrate, thawed

1 cup orange juice

½ cup milk

½ teaspoon pure vanilla extract

2 cups ice cubes

2 ounces (½ baking bar) Ghirardelli Semi-Sweet Chocolate

Place two 16-ounce glasses in the freezer to chill.

In a blender, combine the orange concentrate and juice, milk, vanilla extract, and ice. Blend on high until well-mixed, approximately 1 minute. Add chocolate and blend until chocolate flecks are well distributed throughout. Transfer cooler mixture to chilled glasses and serve immediately.

Pictured opposite page (left)

Mexican Mocha Hot Chocolate

YIELD: TWO 8-OUNCE SERVINGS

1½ cups milk

2 tablespoons Ghirardelli Sweet Ground Chocolate and Cocoa

1 tablespoon powdered instant espresso

Pinch ground cinnamon

¼ cup Sweetened Whipped Cream (page 52), for garnish

2 6-inch-long sticks cinnamon

Heat milk in a small saucepan over medium-high heat, whisking continuously until heated. (Alternatively, heat the milk in a microwave-safe bowl in the microwave on high for 1½ to 2 minutes.)

In a medium-sized bowl, combine the hot milk, ground chocolate, instant espresso, and ground cinnamon, mixing until well blended. Pour the beverage into a tall mug and top with the whipped cream. Place the cinnamon stick in the mug as you would insert a straw and serve immediately.

Pictured opposite page (right)

Chocolate Soda Cooler

YIELD: TWO 12-OUNCE SERVINGS

2 cups cold sparkling water
¼ cup Ghirardelli Sweet Ground Chocolate and Cocoa
½ teaspoon pure vanilla extract
3 scoops vanilla ice cream

Place two 12-ounce glasses in the freezer to chill.

In a blender, combine the sparkling water, ground chocolate, vanilla extract, and 1 scoop of the ice cream. Blend on high until thoroughly mixed. Place 1 scoop of ice cream in each of the chilled glasses and pour in the chocolate mixture, filling the glasses. Serve immediately.

Chocolate Irish Coffee

YIELD: TWO 10-OUNCE SERVINGS

2 cups freshly brewed coffee
¼ cup Ghirardelli Sweet Ground Chocolate and Cocoa
2 tablespoons Irish whiskey
¼ cup Sweetened Whipped Cream (page 52), for garnish
4 teaspoons Créme de menthe, for garnish

Preheat the oven to 250° and place a small mixing bowl inside to warm.

In the warmed bowl, combine the hot coffee, ground chocolate, and Irish whiskey. Stir until well blended. Pour the beverage into glass mugs and top each one with 1 tablespoon of the whipped cream. Drizzle the Créme de menthe over the dollop of whipped cream and serve immediately.

The company that was to become Ghirardelli Chocolate Company outgrew several locations and several names in its first years of operation. It was the "Italian Chocolate Factory" when it came to 415-417 Jackson Street, then it was "Mrs. Ghirardelli & Company" for a short period, perhaps in celebration of the arrival of the founder's wife and family from Peru. Later, the family's expansion was reflected in a new name that proudly included ". . . & Sons."

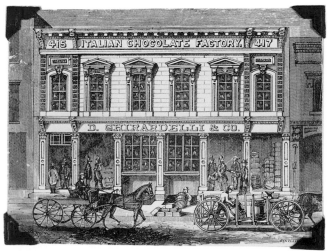

Frosted Chocolate-Banana Yogurt Drink

YIELD: EIGHT 8-OUNCE SERVINGS

½ cup sugar
¼ cup Ghirardelli Sweet Ground Chocolate and Cocoa
1½ cups evaporated skim milk
1 medium banana
Juice from ½ lemon
8 ounces vanilla yogurt
1 teaspoon pure vanilla extract
8 fresh whole strawberries for garnish

Place eight 8-ounce glasses in the freezer to chill.

In a heavy saucepan, combine the sugar and ground chocolate. Add the evaporated milk and stir. Bring the mixture to a boil, whisking until smooth. Refrigerate until slightly chilled, about 30 minutes.

Mash the banana with the lemon juice. Remove the evaporated milk mixture from the refrigerator and stir in the yogurt, banana, and vanilla extract. Chill slightly, approximately 30 minutes. Pour the mixture into a 1-quart freezer container. Cover and freeze until the mixture has become slushy.

Spoon the mixture into chilled glasses, garnish with the strawberries, and serve immediately.

By the time he sat for his portrait photograph, Domingo Ghirardelli was every inch the patriarch and man of substance he appears to be. It takes imagination to see behind the imposing visage to the restless young adventurer who set up shop in a gold rush tent; the man-about-town who rode with the vigilantes to impose order on the new city of San Francisco; the gambler who risked everything on his own judgment—not once, but many times—and won. Domingo Ghirardelli may also have been more of a gourmand than his contemporaries suspected: it's said that when the figs on a prized tree in his garden were almost ripe, he would climb the tree and insert one drop of olive oil in each fig, insisting it made them sweeter and gave them a richer flavor.

25

it's
already
Ground
ready
for you

Easy!

Cakes and Tortes

Chocolate-Almond Layered Cheesecake

YIELD: 16 SERVINGS

CRUST

⅔ **cup almonds, finely chopped**

1¼ **cups finely crushed vanilla wafers**

⅓ **cup butter, melted**

FILLING

8 ounces (2 baking bars) Ghirardelli Bittersweet Chocolate, broken into 1-inch pieces

8 ounces cream cheese, softened

1 cup sugar

3 eggs

1 cup sour cream

¼ **cup almond-flavored liqueur**

¼ **teaspoon salt (optional)**

Preheat the oven to 350°. Grease a 9-inch springform pan.

Place the almonds on a baking sheet and toast in the preheated oven for 3 to 4 minutes. Allow almonds to cool. Place the toasted almonds in a food processor, and process until finely ground. Combine the wafer crumbs, ground almonds, and butter; mix well. Press the mixture onto the bottom of the springform pan and 1½ inches up the sides. Bake 8 minutes. Place on a wire rack and let cool completely.

To prepare the filling, melt the chocolate in a double boiler over hot, but not boiling, water. Stir occasionally until the chocolate is smooth. Set aside.

In a medium-sized mixing bowl, beat the cream cheese on low just until smooth. Gradually add the sugar and continue beating until smooth. Scrape down the sides of the bowl and beaters with a rubber spatula. Add the eggs, one at a time, beating well after each addition and scraping down the bowl as needed. With the mixer on low, gradually add the sour cream, almond liqueur, and salt, beating just until smooth.

Divide the batter in half. Add the melted chocolate to one half of the batter, stirring until smooth. Pour the chocolate batter into the crust; spread to create one even layer. Carefully spoon the plain batter on top of the chocolate batter. Place the pan in the oven and immediately reduce the temperature to 325°. Bake 50 to 60 minutes, or until the center is just set. Turn off the oven, and leave the cake inside for 30 minutes with the oven door closed. Transfer the cheesecake to a wire rack. Loosen it from the sides of the pan with a metal spatula. Let the cheesecake cool completely, then chill it at least 8 hours or overnight. Store covered in the refrigerator.

Pictured opposite page

Chocolate Sour Cream Cake

YIELD: 12 SERVINGS

2 ounces (½ baking bar) Ghirardelli Semi-Sweet Chocolate, broken into 1-inch pieces

1 cup flour

¾ teaspoon baking powder

½ teaspoon baking soda

¼ teaspoon salt (optional)

⅓ cup butter, softened

⅓ cup granulated sugar

⅓ cup packed brown sugar

1 egg, beaten

1 egg yolk, beaten

1 teaspoon pure vanilla extract

½ cup sour cream

½ cup confectioners' sugar

Preheat the oven to 350°. Line a 9-inch round cake pan with waxed paper.

Place the chocolate pieces in a double boiler and melt over hot, but not boiling, water. Stir occasionally until chocolate is smooth. Set aside.

In a small bowl, sift together the flour, baking powder, baking soda, and salt. Set aside.

In a large mixing bowl, cream the butter, granulated sugar, and brown sugar until fluffy. Beat in the whole egg, the egg yolk, and the vanilla extract. Stir in the sour cream. Alternating, add the flour mixture and chocolate mixture to the butter mixture and mix well. Spread the batter into the prepared pan, and bake 30 to 35 minutes, or until a tester comes out clean when inserted into the center of the cake.

Cool the cake on a wire rack for 10 to 15 minutes. Run a knife around the edge of the cake and remove it from the pan. Discard the waxed paper. Let the cake cool completely, then dust with the confectioners' sugar.

Chocolate Decadence Cake

YIELD: 12 TO 16 SERVINGS

BATTER

**12 ounces (3 baking bars) Ghirardelli Bittersweet Chocolate,
broken into 1-inch pieces**

$^1/_2$ cup butter

8 eggs, separated

$^1/_2$ cup sugar

1 teaspoon pure vanilla extract

Pinch salt

DARK CHOCOLATE GLAZE

4 ounces (1 baking bar) Ghirardelli Sweet Dark Chocolate

3 tablespoons butter

1 tablespoon milk

1 tablespoon light corn syrup

$^1/_4$ teaspoon pure vanilla extract

$^1/_3$ cup ground or finely chopped almonds or walnuts

Preheat the oven to 350°. Butter the bottom of a 9-inch springform pan. Line the bottom of the pan with parchment paper. Butter the parchment paper.

Melt the chocolate and butter in a double boiler over hot, but not boiling, water. Stir occasionally until smooth, then remove from the heat and set aside.

Combine the egg yolks, 2 tablespoons of the sugar, the vanilla extract, and salt, and beat lightly until well combined. Add the egg mixture to the chocolate, one tablespoon at a time, whisking continuously. In a separate bowl, combine the egg whites and the 6 remaining tablespoons of sugar and whip until soft peaks form. Transfer the chocolate mixture to a large bowl, pour the egg white mixture on top, and carefully fold it in. (Do not overmix.)

Spread the batter in the prepared pan. Bake on the lower shelf of the preheated oven for 30 to 35 minutes, or until cracked on top and a tester comes out clean when inserted into the center of the cake. Transfer to a wire rack to cool. (Cake will shrink down as it cools.) Remove the pan and discard the parchment paper.

To make the frosting, melt the dark chocolate and butter in a double boiler over hot, but not boiling, water. Stir occasionally until smooth, then remove from the heat. Stir in the milk, syrup, and vanilla extract.

Place the cake layer (still on the rack) over a baking sheet. When the glaze has cooled, pour onto the center of the cake and let it run down the sides. Use a spatula to smooth glaze and coat the sides. Decorate the sides of the cake by pressing the nuts into the glaze. Transfer to the refrigerator and allow glaze to set, approximately 10 minutes.

Classic Cake with Milk Chocolate Frosting

YIELD: 12 SERVINGS

BATTER

½ cup butter, softened

8 ounces cream cheese, softened

2 eggs

2 cups flour

1¼ cups granulated sugar

2 teaspoons baking powder

½ teaspoon baking soda

¼ teaspoon salt (optional)

½ cup milk

1 teaspoon pure vanilla extract

⅓ cup Ghirardelli Semi-Sweet Chocolate Chips

FROSTING

8 ounces (2 baking bars) Ghirardelli Pure Milk Chocolate, broken into 1-inch pieces

3 cups confectioners' sugar

⅔ cup sour cream

2 tablespoons butter, softened

Preheat the oven to 350°. Grease two 8- or 9-inch round cake pans.

In a large bowl, beat the butter and cream cheese until light and fluffy. Add the eggs, one at a time, beating well after each addition. Scrape down the bowl with a rubber spatula. Add the flour, granulated sugar, baking powder, baking soda, salt, milk, and vanilla extract and beat on low until dry ingredients are moistened. Increase the mixing speed to medium and beat 2 minutes. Fold in the chocolate chips. Pour half the batter into each of the two prepared pans, spreading it evenly.

Bake 25 to 30 minutes, or until a tester comes out clean when inserted into the center of the cake and the cake springs back when pressed lightly. Cool the cake in pans on a wire rack for 10 minutes. Run a knife around the edge of the cake and remove from the pan. Transfer to the wire rack and let cool completely.

Meanwhile, make the frosting. Melt the milk chocolate in a double boiler over hot, but not boiling, water. Stir occasionally until the chocolate is smooth.

In a mixing bowl, beat the confectioners' sugar, sour cream, and butter on medium until well blended. Add the melted chocolate and continue to beat on medium for 5 minutes, occasionally scraping the sides of the bowl. Frost the cake. Store tightly covered in the refrigerator.

Double-Dutch Chocolate Pudding Cake

YIELD: 6 SERVINGS

BATTER

¾ *cup flour*

¼ *cup Ghirardelli Sweet Ground Chocolate and Cocoa*

¼ *cup granulated sugar*

1 teaspoon baking powder

¼ *teaspoon salt (optional)*

½ *cup milk*

¼ *cup butter, melted*

1 teaspoon pure vanilla extract

PUDDING

¼ *cup Ghirardelli Sweet Ground Chocolate and Cocoa*

¼ *cup granulated sugar*

¼ *cup firmly packed brown sugar*

1½ *cups boiling water*

Preheat the oven to 350°. Grease an 8-inch square baking pan.

Combine the flour, ¼ cup ground chocolate, ¼ cup granulated sugar, baking powder, and salt. In a separate bowl, combine the milk, butter, and vanilla extract. Add the milk mixture to the dry ingredients and mix well. Pour batter into the prepared pan.

To make the pudding, combine the remaining ¼ cup each of ground chocolate and granulated sugar, the brown sugar, and the boiling water, mixing well. Pour the chocolate mixture over the batter in the pan. (Do not stir.) Bake 35 to 40 minutes, or until the top appears dry. Let stand 30 minutes before serving.

Note: Serve with Sweetened Whipped Cream (page 52) or ice cream, if desired.

Chocolate Ice Cream Cake

YIELD: 12 SERVINGS

BATTER

1 cup milk

¼ cup butter, softened

1 egg

¾ cup granulated sugar

1 teaspoon pure vanilla extract

1¼ teaspoons baking powder

½ teaspoon salt

¼ teaspoon baking soda

¼ cup Ghirardelli Sweet Ground Chocolate and Cocoa

1⅓ cups flour

1 quart vanilla ice cream, softened

FROSTING

4 ounces (1 baking bar) Ghirardelli Unsweetened Chocolate

⅔ cup butter

2 cups confectioners' sugar

⅓ cup milk

1½ teaspoons pure vanilla extract

GLAZE

⅔ cup evaporated milk

½ cup sweetened condensed milk

1 cup Ghirardelli Semi-Sweet Chocolate Chips

½ teaspoon pure vanilla extract

Preheat the oven to 250°. Grease and flour an 8½-inch springform pan.

Combine the milk, butter, egg, granulated sugar, and vanilla extract. Using an electric mixer, beat the ingredients until light and fluffy. In a separate bowl, combine the baking powder, salt, baking soda, ground chocolate, and flour, mixing until blended. Add the dry ingredients to the liquid ingredients. Pour the batter into the prepared pan and bake for 40 to 45 minutes, or until a tester comes out clean when inserted into the center of the cake. (Place aluminum foil under the pan to prevent batter from dripping onto the oven floor.) Cool the cake on a rack for 15 minutes. Transfer the cake to the freezer.

When the cake is frozen, soften the ice cream at room temperature for 15 to 20 minutes (or microwave on high for 10 to 15 seconds). Spoon the ice cream on top of the frozen cake. Smooth the ice cream, using a spatula that has been dipped in hot water, to create an even layer. Place the cake in the freezer.

To make the frosting, melt the unsweetened chocolate in a double boiler over hot, but not boiling, water. Stir the chocolate occasionally until smooth. In a large mixing bowl, beat the butter until fluffy. Gradually add the confectioners' sugar, milk, and vanilla extract to the bowl; mix until smooth. Add the melted chocolate and stir well. Set aside.

Remove the cake from the freezer. Wrap a hot, wet towel around the sides of the pan for 5 minutes. Run a thin, sharp knife around the edges of the pan to loosen the cake; remove the sides. Place the cake on a baking sheet or serving dish and return to the freezer.

Prepare the glaze by combining the evaporated and condensed milk in a double boiler over hot, but not boiling, water and stir. When the milk is warm, add the chocolate chips; stir continuously. When the chocolate has melted and the mixture has thickened, remove it from the heat. Add the vanilla extract and cool slightly.

Place the frozen cake on a wire rack over a baking sheet. Frost the top of the cake with the frosting. (Seal the ice cream completely with the frosting.) Place the cake in the freezer for approximately 1 hour.

Remove the cake from the freezer. Pour the glaze over the frosting; use a spatula to evenly coat the cake. Freeze the cake for 2 to 4 hours or overnight.

*D*omingo Ghirardelli Jr. was a member of the commission that produced the Panama Exposition in 1915 to celebrate the opening of the Panama Canal. As befitted the company's stature, the Ghirardelli exhibition was one of the most elaborate. The Exposition was held in the Marina District, where the Palace of Fine Arts building still stands as an example of the event's architectural extravagances.

Devil's Food Cake with Mocha Buttercream Frosting

YIELD: 12 SERVINGS

BATTER

2 cups flour

1½ cups Ghirardelli Sweet Ground Chocolate and Cocoa

1 cup granulated sugar

1 teaspoon baking soda

½ teaspoon cream of tartar

½ teaspoon salt (optional)

1½ cups buttermilk

1 cup butter, softened

4 eggs

1 teaspoon pure vanilla extract

FROSTING

4 ounces (1 baking bar) Ghirardelli Unsweetened Chocolate, broken into 1-inch pieces

2 teaspoons granulated instant coffee

2 tablespoons boiling water

⅔ cup butter

2 cups confectioners' sugar

⅓ cup milk

1½ teaspoons pure vanilla extract

Preheat the oven to 350°. Grease the bottoms of two 8- or 9-inch round cake pans and line with waxed paper. In a large mixing bowl, combine the flour, ground chocolate, granulated sugar, baking soda, cream of tartar, and salt. Add 1 cup of the buttermilk and the butter. Beat on medium for 2 minutes. Add the remaining ½ cup of buttermilk, the eggs, and the vanilla extract. Divide the batter evenly between the two prepared pans. Bake 30 to 45 minutes, or until a tester comes out clean when inserted into the cake's center. Cool on a wire rack for 10 to 15 minutes. Remove cakes from the pans, discard the waxed paper, and transfer them to the wire rack to cool completely.

To make the frosting, melt the chocolate pieces in a double boiler over hot, but not boiling, water. Stir occasionally until the chocolate is smooth. Dissolve the instant coffee granules in the boiling water. Stir the coffee mixture into the chocolate, remove from the heat, and set aside. In a large mixing bowl, beat the butter until fluffy. Gradually add the confectioners' sugar, milk, and vanilla extract, mixing until smooth. Add the melted chocolate and mix until well combined. Frost the cake.

Pictured opposite page

Chocolate Praline Cheesecake

YIELD: 16 SERVINGS

CRUST

1¼ cups finely crushed chocolate graham cracker crumbs

4 tablespoons butter, melted

FILLING

10 ounces (2½ baking bars) Ghirardelli Semi-Sweet
Chocolate, broken into 1-inch pieces

24 ounces cream cheese, softened

1 cup firmly packed brown sugar

3 eggs

1 cup heavy whipping cream

2 teaspoons pure vanilla extract

¼ teaspoon salt (optional)

TOPPING

½ cup ready-made caramel topping

½ cup chopped pecans

2 ounces (½ baking bar) Ghirardelli Semi-Sweet Chocolate,
coarsely chopped

Preheat the oven to 350°.

In a large bowl, combine the graham cracker crumbs and butter; mix well. Press the crumbs evenly onto the bottom of an ungreased 9-inch springform pan. Bake for 8 minutes. Cool completely on a wire rack.

Melt 10 ounces of the chocolate in a double boiler over hot, but not boiling, water. Stir the chocolate occasionally until smooth. Remove from the heat.

In a large bowl, beat the cream cheese on low just until smooth. Gradually add the brown sugar and continue beating until smooth. Scrape down the sides of the bowl and the beaters with a rubber spatula. Add the eggs, one at a time, beating well after each addition and scraping down the bowl as needed. Beat in the melted chocolate until smooth. Add the whipping cream, vanilla extract, and salt, beating just until smooth. Pour the filling into the crust and place the cake in the oven. Immediately lower the oven temperature to 325°.

Bake 1 hour to 1 hour 10 minutes, or until the center is just set. Turn off the oven, and leave the cake inside for 30 minutes with the oven door closed. Transfer the cake to a wire rack. Using a metal spatula, loosen the cake from the sides of the pan.

To make the topping, reheat the oven to 350°. Place the chopped pecans on a baking sheet and toast for 3 to 4 minutes, or until fragrant. Combine the caramel topping, toasted pecans, and remaining 2 ounces of chocolate. Spoon the mixture over the warm cake. After the cake has cooled completely, chill it for at least 8 hours, or overnight. Store covered in the refrigerator.

Chocolate Carrot Cake

YIELD: 16 SERVINGS

BATTER

1²⁄₃ cups granulated sugar

1½ cups vegetable oil

4 eggs

2½ cups flour

²⁄₃ cup Ghirardelli Sweet Ground Chocolate and Cocoa

1 teaspoon baking soda

1 teaspoon salt (optional)

½ teaspoon ground cinnamon

2½ cups firmly packed shredded carrots

¾ cup finely chopped walnuts

2 teaspoons grated orange peel

FROSTING

6 ounces cream cheese, softened

2 tablespoons milk

1 teaspoon pure vanilla extract

2 cups confectioners' sugar

Preheat the oven to 350°. Grease the bottom of a 9 x 13-inch baking pan.

In a large mixing bowl, combine the granulated sugar and oil. Add the eggs, one at a time, beating well after each addition. In a separate bowl, combine the flour, ground chocolate, baking soda, salt, and cinnamon. Gradually add the dry ingredients to the sugar-egg mixture, mixing until well combined. Stir in the carrots, nuts, and orange peel. Transfer the batter to the prepared pan, spreading it evenly. Bake 45 to 50 minutes, or until a tester comes out clean when inserted into the center of the cake. Let the cake cool completely.

To make the frosting, combine the cream cheese, milk, and vanilla, beating until smooth. Gradually add the confectioners' sugar, and continue to beat until well blended. Spread on top of the cake. Store covered in the refrigerator.

Eagles and parrots were the first symbols used for Ghirardelli chocolate advertisements and labels. Domingo Ghirardelli briefly used the name "Eagle Chocolate Company" in 1882, and the eagle stayed on as a permanent part of the logo. Domingo finally settled on his family name for the company. This created problems, though, for those unfamiliar with Italian pronunciation. No one knows who first thought of using a parrot to teach people how to say "Gear-ar-delly." The device flies in the face of advertising wisdom, which commands that thou shalt not misspell thy company's name, but it has been brilliantly successful in solving the pronunciation problem—and in inspiring artists to various flights of fancy in drawing the bird.

White Mocha Cheesecake

YIELD: 16 SERVINGS

CRUST

4 tablespoons butter, softened

2 tablespoons sugar

6 tablespoons Ghirardelli Sweet Ground Chocolate and
Cocoa

$^1\!/_2$ cup flour

1 teaspoon pure vanilla extract

TOPPING

2 cups (16 ounces) sour cream

$^1\!/_2$ cup sugar

$^1\!/_2$ teaspoon pure vanilla extract

2 tablespoons powdered instant coffee

FILLING

24 ounces cream cheese, softened

2 eggs

$^3\!/_4$ cup sugar

2 tablespoons flour

$^1\!/_2$ teaspoon salt

16 ounces (4 baking bars) Ghirardelli Classic White
Confection, broken into 1-inch pieces

1 cup heavy whipping cream

3 tablespoons instant coffee

Preheat the oven to 400°.

Cream the butter and sugar until fluffy. Using a fork to mix, add the ground chocolate, flour, and vanilla extract. Stir until well blended. Press the mixture evenly onto the bottom of a 9-inch springform pan. Bake 10 to 12 minutes, or until golden brown. Cool completely on a wire rack.

To prepare the topping, combine the sour cream, sugar, and vanilla extract. Transfer half of the mixture to a separate bowl, and whisk in the instant coffee. Mix well and refrigerate.

While the topping chills, prepare the filling. Preheat the oven to 375°. In a large mixing bowl, blend the cream cheese just until smooth. Add the eggs, one at a time, beating well after each addition and scraping down the bowl as needed with a rubber spatula. In a small bowl, combine the sugar, flour, and salt. Add the dry ingredients to the cream cheese mixture and blend just until smooth.

Place the white confection pieces in a double boiler over hot, but not boiling, water. Stir occasionally until the chocolate is smooth. Gradually pour the chocolate into the cream cheese mixture and mix to combine. Stir in the whipping cream. Transfer 1 ½ cups batter to a separate bowl and whisk in the instant coffee. (The coffee granules may not dissolve completely.)

Pour the remaining filling into the cooled crust.

Drop rounded teaspoonfuls of the coffee mixture into the cheese filling, creating 5 wells. Swirl 2 to 3 times with the tip of a butter knife to create a marbled effect.

Bake 55 minutes to 1 hour. Remove the cheesecake from the oven and immediately run a knife around the edge of the cake to loosen it from the sides of the pan.

Pour the chilled topping and the remaining coffee topping on top of the cheesecake. Using the tip of a butter knife, carefully create a swirl effect with the toppings. Bake the cheesecake 5 to 7 minutes to set the topping. Remove from the oven and cool on a wire rack for 1 hour. Refrigerate at least 4 hours before serving. Store covered in the refrigerator.

Note: Although cheesecakes freeze very well, sour cream toppings do not. If freezing this cheesecake, bake and cool completely. Cover or wrap well and freeze. Remove the day or several hours before serving and defrost in the refrigerator. Prepare topping as directed.

When sacks of cocoa beans arrive from far-off equatorial lands, test samples are chosen at random. The beans are lined up on a tray and sliced through the center with surgical precision in a "cut test," then carefully examined by Ghirardelli experts. One of the things they are looking for is any trace of purple in the middle of the beans. Finding purple would mean the beans hadn't been thoroughly fermented—a process done before shipment to remove the bitterness of raw beans and develop their chocolate flavor and deep brown color. If any purple is found, the shipment is rejected. The art of selecting and tasting the cocoa beans and the science of meticulous roasting and processing are both necessary to produce a superior chocolate.

Three-Tiered Chocolate-Almond Torte

YIELD: 12 SERVINGS

BATTER

$1^1/_2$ cups flour

$^1/_2$ cup Ghirardelli Sweet Ground Chocolate and Cocoa

1 teaspoon baking powder

$1^1/_4$ cups granulated sugar

6 eggs

$^1/_4$ cup butter, melted

FROSTING

4 ounces (1 baking bar) Ghirardelli Bittersweet Chocolate, broken into 1-inch pieces

$^1/_2$ cup almonds, finely chopped

$^2/_3$ cup butter, softened

$1^1/_4$ cups confectioners' sugar

1 teaspoon pure vanilla extract

GLAZE

4 ounces (1 baking bar) Ghirardelli Bittersweet Chocolate, broken into 1-inch pieces

$^1/_4$ cup light corn syrup

$^1/_4$ cup butter, softened

Preheat the oven to 350°. Grease three 9-inch round cake pans; line with waxed paper. Lightly grease the waxed paper.

Combine the flour, ground chocolate, and baking powder; set aside. In a large bowl, beat the granulated sugar and eggs on medium approximately 5 minutes, or until light and doubled in volume. Blend in the butter until smooth. Slowly blend in the flour mixture until smooth. Divide batter evenly among the prepared pans.

Place the pans in the oven, staggering them (two pans should be close to the sides of the top rack and the third pan should be in the center of the lower rack). Bake 8 to 10 minutes, or until a tester comes out clean when inserted into the center of each cake. Run a knife around the edge of the cakes, and immediately turn them out onto wire cooling racks. Remove the waxed paper, and cool completely.

To make the frosting, melt 4 ounces of the bittersweet chocolate pieces in a double boiler over hot, but not boiling, water. Stir occasionally until smooth.

Place the almonds on a baking sheet and toast at 350° for 3 to 4 minutes. Let the nuts cool. *(Continued)*

Pictured opposite page

This etching from 1915 shows the Ghirardelli block just before the Clock Tower was added. The Panama Exposition is in full swing at the upper left, complete with Ferris wheel and gala pennants streaming in the wind. The wind also catches smoke from the Ghirardelli powerhouse; at the lower right, a team of dray horses hauls sacks of raw cocoa beans just in from South America, while around the corner along North Point Street another team loads finished chocolate. A few horseless carriages give the final touch of modernity to this picture of bustling industry and proud prosperity.

In a small bowl, beat the butter until light and fluffy. Slowly beat in the confectioner's sugar and vanilla extract. beat in the chocolate until smooth. stir in all but 2 tablespoons of the toasted almonds. Set aside the reserved almonds. Cut four 3-inch-wide strips of waxed paper and arrange in a square on the serving plate (to catch the excess glaze).

Place one of the cake layers on the square of waxed paper strips, and top with half of the frosting. Repeat with the second layer and the remaining frosting. Top with the remaining layer.

To make the glaze, melt the remaining 4 ounces of bittersweet chocolate pieces in a double boiler as directed for the frosting. Stir in the corn syrup and butter until smooth. Immediately pour the mixture over the top of the torte. Spread the glaze evenly on the sides of the torte. garnish the top with the remaining 2 tablespoons of almonds. Let stand for 30 minutes at room temperature to set the glaze.

Note: This recipe may also be prepared in a 15 x 10-inch jelly-roll pan. Grease and line the jelly-roll pan as directed above. Bake at 350°for 14 to 15 minutes, or until a tester comes out clean when inserted into the center of the cake. When the cake is cool, cut it into three 10 x 5-inch rectangles, then frost and glaze as directed.

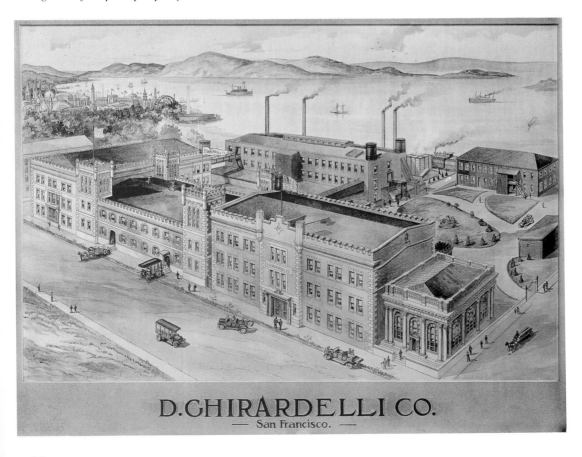

D. GHIRARDELLI CO.
— San Francisco. —

Upside-Down German Chocolate Cake

YIELD: 9 SERVINGS

TOPPING

²⁄₃ **cup firmly packed brown sugar**

¹⁄₃ **cup butter, cut into small pieces**

3 **tablespoons heavy whipping cream**

¹⁄₃ **cup coarsely chopped pecans**

¹⁄₄ **cup flaked coconut**

BATTER

2 **ounces (¹⁄₂ baking bar) Ghirardelli Sweet Dark Chocolate, broken into 1-inch pieces**

1 **cup granulated sugar**

¹⁄₂ **cup butter, softened**

2 **eggs**

¹⁄₂ **teaspoon pure vanilla extract**

1 **cup flour**

¹⁄₂ **teaspoon baking soda**

Pinch salt (optional)

¹⁄₂ **cup buttermilk**

¹⁄₄ **cup water**

Preheat the oven to 350°. Grease an 8- or a 9-inch square baking pan.

In a small heavy saucepan, combine the brown sugar, butter, and whipping cream. Cook the mixture over low heat until the butter melts, stirring occasionally. Remove from the heat. Stir in the pecans and coconut. Spread onto the bottom of the prepared pan. Set aside.

Melt the chocolate in a double boiler over hot, but not boiling, water. Stir occasionally until the chocolate is smooth. Set aside.

In a large mixing bowl, cream the granulated sugar and butter on medium until fluffy. Beat in the eggs. Stir in the melted chocolate and vanilla extract. In a separate bowl, combine the flour, baking soda, and salt. In another bowl, combine the buttermilk and water. Alternately, add the flour mixture and the buttermilk mixture to the large mixing bowl, stirring well after each addition. Pour over the topping in the pan.

Bake for 40 to 45 minutes, or until a tester comes out clean when inserted into the center of the cake. Cool in the pan on a wire rack for 10 minutes. Run a knife around the edge of the cake; invert the pan onto a serving plate. Cool cake completely before serving. Store tightly covered.

Note: Sour milk may be substituted for buttermilk. To make sour milk for this recipe, place 1½ teaspoons white vinegar or lemon juice in a measuring cup and add milk to equal ½ cup in total. Stir, and let stand for 5 minutes.

Flourless Mocha Torte

YIELD: 8 SERVINGS

BATTER

6 ounces (1½ baking bars) Ghirardelli Bittersweet Chocolate, broken into 1-inch pieces

1 tablespoon instant freeze-dried coffee

3 tablespoons boiling water

6 eggs, separated

⅔ cup sugar

¼ teaspoon salt (optional)

FROSTING

4 ounces (1 baking bar) Ghirardelli Pure Milk Chocolate, broken into 1-inch pieces

1 tablespoon instant freeze-dried coffee

¼ cup boiling water

2 cups heavy whipping cream

1 ounce (¼ baking bar) Ghirardelli Bittersweet Chocolate shavings (page 18)

Melt the bittersweet chocolate in a double boiler over hot, but not boiling, water. Stir occasionally until the chocolate is smooth. Set aside.

Dissolve the coffee in boiling water; set aside. Preheat the oven to 350°. Grease two 8- or 9-inch round cake pans. Line the bottom of the pans with waxed paper, and grease the waxed paper. In a large mixing bowl, whip the egg whites on medium until soft peaks form. With the mixer running, gradually add ⅓ cup sugar. Increase the mixing speed to high and continue beating until stiff peaks form. (The meringue should be shiny.) In another large bowl, whip the yolks, the remaining ⅓ cup sugar, and the salt until thick and lemon colored, approximately 5 minutes. Slowly add the chocolate and coffee; beat until well blended. Gently fold ¼ of the egg whites into the yolk mixture to lighten it. Carefully but thoroughly fold in the remaining whites until no streaks remain.

Pour the batter into the prepared pans. Bake on the center oven rack for 25 minutes. Turn off the oven and leave the cake inside for 5 minutes with the oven door closed. Transfer the pans to a wire rack (the centers will fall). Remove the waxed paper while the cake is warm. Cool completely.

For the frosting, melt the chocolate as directed for the cake. Dissolve the coffee in boiling water; add all at once to the chocolate, stirring continuously until smooth. Cool completely. In a large mixing bowl, beat the whipping cream at high speed until stiff peaks form. Gently fold the chocolate mixture into the whipped cream.

To assemble the torte, level the top of each layer by cutting off the raised edges with a long serrated knife. Place one layer on a serving plate. Spread the layer with 1 cup of the chocolate whipped cream. Top with the remaining cake layer. Frost the top and sides of the torte with the remaining frosting. Sprinkle the top with chocolate shavings. ***Pictured opposite page***

an All-purpose CHOCOLATE !

Pies
and
Tarts

Classic Pie Crust

YIELD: ONE 9- OR 10-INCH PIE CRUST

1 cup flour
½ teaspoon salt
⅓ cup vegetable shortening
1½ teaspoons butter
2 tablespoons ice water

In a large mixing bowl, combine the flour and salt. Using a pastry blender or fork, cut the shortening and butter into the flour mixture until it resembles small peas. Sprinkle the ice water over the mixture.

Using your fingers, work the dough gently just until it starts to pull away from the sides of the bowl and can be formed into a ball. (Add 1 additional tablespoon of ice water if the dough doesn't adhere well.) Wrap and refrigerate the dough at least 1 hour.

Roll the dough on a lightly floured surface to form a 10-inch circle, approximately ⅛ inch thick. (Roll dough into an 11-inch circle to make a 10-inch pie crust.) Line a 9-inch pie plate with the dough. (Pastry should extend ⅛ inch beyond the edge of the pie plate). Crimp the edges or press with a fork to create a decorative pattern. Place the pie plate in the refrigerator and allow to chill, approximately 15 minutes.

To pre-bake the crust, preheat the oven to 450°. Prick the bottom and sides of the crust with the tines of a fork, at ½-inch intervals, to prevent bubbles from forming while baking. Bake 8 to 10 minutes, or until light golden brown. Cool on a wire rack.

Crunchy Mud Pie

YIELD: 8 SERVINGS

CRUST

1 ½ cups chocolate sandwich cookies, crushed

4 tablespoons butter, melted

FILLING

4 ounces (1 baking bar) Ghirardelli Sweet Dark Chocolate, broken into 1-inch pieces

½ cup chocolate sandwich cookies, crushed

1½ quarts chocolate or coffee ice cream, softened

3 tablespoons heavy whipping cream

1 tablespoon butter

1 teaspoon powdered instant coffee

1 teaspoon boiling water

Preheat the oven to 325°. Coat the inside of a 9-inch pie pan with nonstick cooking spray.

Place the crushed cookies in a food processor or blender, and finely grind. In a medium-sized bowl, combine 1½ cups of the finely ground cookie crumbs with 4 tablespoons of the butter, mixing well. Spoon the mixture into prepared pan. Using your fingers or the back of a spoon, pat the mixture into the bottom and up the sides of the pan. Bake the crust for 7 minutes. Cool completely on a wire rack. Freeze for 30 minutes.

Meanwhile, melt 2 ounces of the chocolate in a double boiler over hot, but not boiling, water. Stir the chocolate occasionally until smooth. Stir in the remaining ½ cup of finely ground cookies.

Spread the chocolate mixture in a thin layer on a waxed paper–covered baking sheet. Freeze for 15 minutes, then peel the chocolate off the paper and transfer it to a cutting board. Chop the chocolate coarsely, then place it in a bowl and refrigerate.

Remove the crust from the freezer and spread the softened ice cream into the frozen crust. Return it, uncovered, to the freezer.

In a heavy saucepan, bring the whipping cream just to a boil. Remove the pan from the heat. Stir in the remaining 2 ounces of chocolate. Cover the pan. Let the chocolate cream stand approximately 5 minutes, or until melted. Add the remaining 1 tablespoon of butter and stir until smooth. In a small bowl, dissolve the coffee in the boiling water, and stir into the saucepan.

Remove the filled pie from the freezer and sprinkle it with the chilled cookie crumb mixture. Drizzle the sauce over the pie. Freeze for at least 2 hours, or until the ice cream is firm. Before serving, let the pie stand at room temperature for 15 minutes. The pie may be stored up to 5 days in the freezer, covered tightly.

Note: Ice cream may be softened in a microwave oven on high for 10 to 15 seconds.

This "shelf talker" is one of the advertising pieces created for Ghirardelli. Its plain, homey design may be a product of a simpler, less sophisticated time, but you can almost smell the hot cocoa in the plain white teacup, and the no-nonsense message beautifully expresses the company's confidence in one of its signature products. Simple and modest as the piece may be, its claim is loud and clear: We were the first, and we are the best.

Layered Chocolate Pie with Chocolate Curls

YIELD: 8 SERVINGS

4 ounces (1 baking bar) Ghirardelli Bittersweet Chocolate, broken into 1-inch pieces

8 ounces cream cheese, softened

1½ cups heavy whipping cream

1½ cups confectioners' sugar

4 ounces (1 baking bar) Ghirardelli Pure Milk Chocolate, broken into 1-inch pieces

1 9-inch baked Classic Pie Crust (page 50), or 1 ready-made pie crust

1 3.4-ounce package vanilla-flavored instant pudding and pie-filling mix

1¼ cups milk

SWEETENED WHIPPED CREAM

½ cup heavy whipping cream

2 teaspoons confectioners' sugar

2 ounces Ghirardelli Bittersweet Chocolate curls (page 18), for garnish

Melt the bittersweet chocolate in a double boiler over hot, but not boiling, water. Stir occasionally until the chocolate is smooth. Set aside.

In a small mixing bowl, beat the cream cheese on high for approximately 1 minute. Add ½ cup of the whipping cream and the confectioners' sugar; beat on high for 1 minute. Stir in the melted chocolate. Pour the mixture into the crust. Chill for 1 hour.

Melt the milk chocolate in a double boiler over hot, but not boiling, water. In a medium mixing bowl, combine the pudding mix and milk. Beat on low just until blended, then beat on high 2 minutes. Add the melted chocolate and continue to beat on high for 1 minute. Set aside.

In a small mixing bowl, whip the remaining 1 cup of whipping cream until stiff peaks form. Fold the whipped cream into the pudding mixture; spread over the cream cheese layer of the pie. Chill the pie for 2 hours.

To make the Sweetened Whipped Cream, combine the ½ cup whipping cream and confectioners' sugar in a mixing bowl, and whip until soft peaks form. Transfer the whipped cream to a pastry bag (see the note for the Meringue Tart, page 64, if you do not have a pastry bag), and decorate the pie as desired. Garnish with the chocolate curls, and serve.

Pictured opposite page

Peanut Butter Chocolate Chunk Pie

YIELD: 8 SERVINGS

8 ounces cream cheese, softened

½ cup creamy peanut butter

*3 ounces (¾ baking bar) Ghirardelli Sweet Dark Chocolate,
chopped*

⅔ cup confectioners' sugar

½ teaspoon pure vanilla extract

1 cup heavy whipping cream

1 9-inch baked chocolate cookie-crumb crust (page 51)

*1 ounce (¼ baking bar) Ghirardelli Sweet Dark Chocolate,
broken into 1-inch pieces*

Careful selection, blending, and roasting of the cocoa beans is the key to producing a superior flavor that is uniform from week to week. Today's roasters are more streamlined than those pictured here, but the roasting process has remained almost the same over the decades. The beans vary in color because they are from different countries of origin.

In a small mixing bowl, beat the cream cheese and peanut butter on medium until light and fluffy, approximately 2 minutes. Stir in the chopped chocolate. Add the confectioners' sugar and vanilla extract, mixing until well blended. In a large mixing bowl, whip the whipping cream until stiff peaks form. Fold the cream cheese mixture into the whipped cream. Spoon the mixture into the crust.

Place the chocolate pieces in a double boiler over hot, but not boiling, water; cover and remove from the heat. Let stand approximately 5 minutes. Stir until smooth. If not melted, remove the bowl and return saucepan to the heat. Repeat steps until melted. Drizzle melted chocolate in parallel lines laterally, then vertically to create a crisscross pattern. Chill 2 to 3 hours before serving.

Mocha Cream Pie

YIELD: 8 SERVINGS

CRUST

1½ cups chocolate sandwich cookies, crushed

3 tablespoons butter, melted

FILLING

1 1.75-ounce package unflavored gelatin

¼ cup water

1 tablespoon freeze-dried instant coffee

6 ounces (1½ baking bars) Ghirardelli Sweet Dark Chocolate, broken into 1-inch pieces

½ cup sour cream

1½ cups heavy whipping cream

1 cup confectioners' sugar

2 ounces (½ baking bar) Ghirardelli Sweet Dark Chocolate curls (page 18), for garnish

Preheat the oven to 350°. Place the crumbled cookies in a food processor or blender, and grind finely. In a medium-sized mixing bowl, combine the cookie crumbs and butter, mixing well. Spoon the mixture into a 9-inch glass pie plate. Using your fingers or the back of a spoon, pat the mixture into the bottom and up the sides of the pie plate. Bake 10 minutes. Cool on a wire rack.

To make the filling, stir the gelatin and water in a small saucepan and let it sit for 5 minutes to soften the gelatin. Bring the gelatin to a gentle boil. Add the instant coffee and stir until it has dissolved. Remove from the heat and set aside.

Melt the chocolate in a double boiler over hot, but not boiling, water. Stir occasionally until the chocolate is smooth. Add the sour cream to the coffee mixture, then gradually stir in the melted chocolate. Set aside. In a large bowl, beat the whipping cream on high until soft peaks form. On low, beat in the confectioners' sugar until stiff peaks form. Fold one quarter of the whipped cream into the chocolate mixture (the mixture will be flecked) to lighten. Fold in the remaining whipped cream. Spoon filling into the prepared crust and chill for 2 hours, or until set. While the pie is chilling, make the chocolate curls as the instructions direct. Garnish the pie with the chocolate curls and serve. Store covered in the refrigerator.

Chocolate Pecan Pie

YIELD: 8 TO 10 SERVINGS

6 ounces (1½ baking bars) Ghirardelli Sweet Dark Chocolate,
broken into 1-inch pieces

3 eggs

¾ cup sugar

1 cup light corn syrup

2 tablespoons butter, melted

1 teaspoon pure vanilla extract

¼ teaspoon salt (optional)

1½ cups pecan halves

1 9-inch unbaked Classic Pie Crust (page 50), or
1 ready-made pie crust

1 cup Sweetened Whipped Cream (page 52)

10 chocolate-dipped pecan halves (page 19), for garnish

Preheat the oven to 350°.

Melt the chocolate in a double boiler over hot, but not boiling, water. Stir occasionally until the chocolate is smooth. Set aside.

In a large mixing bowl, beat the eggs. Stir in the sugar. Add the corn syrup, butter, vanilla, and salt, whisking until well blended. Stir in the melted chocolate and pecans. Pour into the prepared crust.

Bake 60 to 65 minutes, or until the center of the pie has set. Cool on a wire rack for 4 hours, or overnight.

Serve the pie at room temperature with the Sweetened Whipped Cream and chocolate-dipped pecan halves.

Note: For a more decorated effect, prepare the pie crust and filling as the recipe directs, but don't add the pecans. Pour the filling into the prepared crust and arrange the pecan halves over the filling in tight concentric circles. Gently press the pecans into the filling to coat them slightly and prevent them from burning while baking. Bake as the recipe directs.

Pictured opposite page

Chocolate-Cherry Custard Pie

YIELD: 12 SERVINGS

1 10-inch unbaked Classic Pie Crust (page 50, and see directions below), or 1 ready-made pie crust

17 ounces canned dark sweet cherries, well drained

1 cup heavy whipping cream

4 ounces (1 baking bar) Ghirardelli Bittersweet Chocolate, broken into 1-inch pieces

2 eggs

½ cup granulated sugar

⅛ teaspoon almond extract

2 tablespoons sliced almonds

¼ cup confectioners' sugar (optional)

Make the pie crust dough as the recipe directs. Place the rolled crust in a 10-inch tart pan and bake as directed.

Reduce the oven temperature to 350°. Using paper towels, pat the cherries dry. Place the cherries on the bottom of the pie shell.

In a heavy saucepan, bring the whipping cream to a boil and immediately remove from the heat. Stir chocolate into the cream, cover, and let stand approximately 5 minutes, or until melted. Stir mixture until smooth, and set aside.

In a medium-sized bowl, combine the eggs, sugar, and almond extract, whisking until well blended. While whisking continuously, add the chocolate mixture. Place the tart shell on the oven rack and carefully pour the chocolate-egg mixture into the crust, covering the cherries. Sprinkle with almonds.

Bake for 25 to 28 minutes, or until set. Cool completely on a wire rack. Just before serving, dust with the confectioners' sugar. Store covered in the refrigerator.

Fudge and Nut Pie

YIELD: 12 SERVINGS

1 10-inch unbaked Classic Pie Crust (page 50, and see directions below), or 1 ready-made crust

8 ounces (2 baking bars) Ghirardelli Semi-Sweet Chocolate, broken into 1-inch pieces

4 eggs

²/₃ cup sugar

½ cup heavy whipping cream or half-and-half

2 tablespoons butter, melted

1 teaspoon pure vanilla extract

¼ teaspoon salt (optional)

1 cup coarsely chopped walnuts, toasted

1 cup coarsely chopped pecans, toasted

Sweetened Whipped Cream (page 52), for garnish

Make the pie crust dough as the recipe directs. Place the rolled crust in a 10-inch tart pan and bake as directed.

Melt the chocolate in a double boiler over hot, but not boiling, water. Stir occasionally until the chocolate is smooth. Set aside.

Reduce the oven temperature to 350°.

In a large mixing bowl, beat the eggs with the sugar until lemon-colored. Beat in the whipping cream, butter, vanilla extract, and salt. Add the melted chocolate and mix until smooth. Stir in the nuts. Pour batter into the prepared crust. Bake 40 to 45 minutes, or until a knife blade comes out clean when inserted into the center of the pie. Serve the pie at room temperature with Sweetened Whipped Cream or ice cream.

Chocolate Hazelnut-Pear Tart

YIELD: 12 SERVINGS

16 ounces canned pear halves, well drained

³/₄ cup sugar

¹/₂ cup butter, softened

2 eggs

2 tablespoons hazelnut-flavored liqueur

¹/₄ teaspoon salt (optional)

1 cup flour

¹/₂ cup Ghirardelli Sweet Ground Chocolate and Cocoa

¹/₂ cup chopped hazelnuts

*2 ounces (¹/₂ baking bar) Ghirardelli Bittersweet Chocolate,
for garnish*

Preheat the oven to 350°. Spray the bottom and sides of a 9-inch springform pan with nonstick cooking spray, or grease lightly.

Pat the pear halves dry with paper towels. Cut each half into thirds lengthwise. Set aside.

Cream the sugar and butter until light and fluffy. Beat in the eggs, liqueur, and salt. In a separate bowl, combine the flour and ground chocolate. Add the dry ingredients to the egg mixture, mixing well. Stir in the nuts. Spread into the prepared pan.

Arrange the pear slices in a circular pattern on top of the batter. Bake 25 to 30 minutes, or until a tester comes out clean when inserted into the center of the tart. Cool tart on a wire rack. When the tart is partly cooled, run a knife around its edge and remove it from the pan. Allow the tart to cool completely.

Melt the bittersweet chocolate in a double boiler over hot, but not boiling, water. Stir the chocolate occasionally until smooth. Using a spoon or pastry bag (see page 20), drizzle the melted chocolate over the cooled tart.

Pictured opposite page

Meringue Fruit Tart

YIELD: 8 SERVINGS

MERINGUE

$^1/_3$ cup finely chopped blanched almonds

3 egg whites

$^1/_4$ teaspoon cream of tartar

$^3/_4$ cup sugar

Dash almond extract

FILLING

1 cup sliced ripe peaches

$1^1/_2$ cups mixed fresh berries, such as blueberries,
strawberries, blackberries, and raspberries

1 tablespoon sugar

4 ounces (1 baking bar) Ghirardelli Sweet Dark Chocolate,
broken into 1-inch pieces

GLAZE

$^1/_3$ cup apricot preserves, strained to remove fruit pieces

$1^1/_2$ teaspoons water

Preheat the oven to 350°. Place the almonds on a baking sheet and toast 3 to 4 minutes. Let the nuts cool and set aside. Lower the oven temperature to 275°. Line a baking sheet with aluminum foil or parchment paper.

In a small mixing bowl, beat the egg whites and cream of tartar on high until foamy. Gradually add the sugar, beating on high until stiff but not dry. Fold in the toasted almonds and almond extract. Transfer the mixture to a pastry bag fitted with a $^1/_2$-inch plain or star tip. In the center of the preparing baking sheet, pipe tight concentric circles, forming a 9-inch round. Build up the outer edge of the circle by piping a second layer on top.

Bake 1 hour, or until light golden brown. Turn off the oven and leave the meringue inside (to dry) for 1 hour with the oven door closed. Transfer tart to a wire rack to cool for 10 minutes, then carefully remove the foil and let the tart cool completely.

To make the filling, combine the peaches, berries, and sugar. Melt the chocolate in a double boiler over hot, but not boiling, water. Stir occasionally until chocolate is smooth. Drizzle half the chocolate over the meringue tart, then top with mixed fruit.

To make the glaze, heat the apricot preserves in a small saucepan over medium heat just until boiling. Stir in the water and remove from the heat. Brush on the glaze immediately, glazing only the peaches and strawberries (blueberries, blackberries, and raspberries are not attractive when glazed), and let stand 15 minutes. Drizzle the remaining melted chocolate over the top of the tart. (Melt the chocolate in the double boiler again if it has hardened.) Serve immediately.   *(continued)*

Pictured opposite page

Note: The meringue shell may be made 3 to 4 days ahead if stored in a warm, dry place. A heavy 1-quart plastic storage bag substituted for a pastry bag. Push the meringue into one of the lower corners of the bag. Cut a small piece off the corner to use as a tip, and squeeze the bag gently to dispense.

At the turn of the century, cocoa bean harvesters relied on the hot South and Central American sun to ferment the beans before they were shipped to customers like Domingo Ghirardelli. Here, the workers rake the beans into thin layers to encourage even fermentation.

Cookies
and
Bars

Milk Chocolate Chip Cookies with Pecans

YIELD: 4 DOZEN

10 ounces (2½ baking bars) Ghirardelli Bittersweet Chocolate, broken into 1-inch pieces

½ cup butter, softened

½ cup granulated sugar

1 cup firmly packed brown sugar

4 eggs

1 teaspoon pure vanilla extract

2¼ cups flour

1 teaspoon baking powder

½ teaspoon baking soda

½ teaspoon salt

1 teaspoon powdered instant espresso

2 cups Ghirardelli Milk Chocolate Chips

1 cup pecans, coarsely chopped

Melt the bittersweet chocolate pieces in a double boiler over hot, but not boiling, water. In a large mixing bowl, cream the butter, granulated sugar, and brown sugar on medium-high until light and fluffy. Reduce mixing speed to low, and add the eggs and vanilla extract. Scrape the bottom and sides of the mixing bowl.

In a separate bowl, sift together the flour, baking powder, baking soda, salt, and espresso powder. Add half the flour mixture to the creamed butter, mixing well. Add half the melted chocolate and stir until ingredients are well blended. Add the remaining flour, incorporating thoroughly, then add the remaining chocolate. Stir in the chocolate chips and pecans. Cover and refrigerate the dough 1 hour.

Preheat the oven to 350°. Line 2 baking sheets with parchment paper. Remove the dough from the refrigerator. Drop the dough in rounded tablespoonfuls onto the prepared baking sheets. Bake 15 to 17 minutes. Upon removing from the oven, immediately slide the parchment paper and cookies onto a wire rack to cool. Store in an airtight container at room temperature or in the freezer.

Pictured opposite page

Trading cards of silent movie stars were a popular promotion premium, capitalizing on America's fascination with the glamorous world of motion pictures. Ghirardelli was one of the companies that packaged cards with the candy they sold in movie theaters in the early 1920s. All the stars on these cards were at the height of their careers at the time Ghirardelli featured them, but only a few survived the introduction of talkies a few years later. Talking movies needed stars who had good voices as well as good looks, and who could handle more sophisticated plots.

Mabel Normand enjoyed tremendous success as Chaplin's co-star in *Tillie's Punctured Romance* in 1914 and in dozens of other silent films. She was born into a vaudeville family, became a fashion model at age thirteen, and started acting in movies by age sixteen. Later, she became notorious for wild living; after she was involved in two murder scandals, her career went downhill. Talkies finished it off.

Black and White Macaroons

YIELD: 4 DOZEN

3 egg whites
¼ teaspoon cream of tartar
¼ teaspoon salt (optional)
1 cup sugar
1 teaspoon pure vanilla extract
2 cups flaked unsweetened coconut
1½ cups Ghirardelli Semi-Sweet Chocolate Chips

Preheat the oven to 300°. Line 2 baking sheets with aluminum foil. In a large bowl, beat the egg whites until foamy. Add the cream of tartar and salt; continue beating until soft peaks form. Gradually add the sugar and vanilla extract, beating until stiff but not dry. Fold in the coconut and 1 cup of the chocolate chips. Drop by rounded teaspoonfuls onto the prepared baking sheets, 1 to 2 inches apart. Sprinkle the cookies with the remaining ½ cup of chocolate chips.

Bake 20 minutes, or until the surfaces begin to crack. Cool completely before removing the cookies from the foil. Store loosely covered at room temperature.

Note: Humidity has an adverse effect on the way meringues are prepared and stored. For best results, make this recipe on cool, clear days.

Double Chocolate Cookies

YIELD: 3½ DOZEN

1¼ cups butter, softened
2 cups sugar
2 eggs
1 tablespoon pure vanilla extract
2 cups flour
1¼ cups Ghirardelli Unsweetened Premium Cocoa
1 teaspoon baking powder
2 cups Ghirardelli Classic White Chips

Preheat the oven to 300°.

In a large mixing bowl, cream the butter and sugar until light and fluffy. Add the eggs one at a time, beating well after each addition, and the vanilla extract. In a separate bowl, combine the flour, ground cocoa, and baking powder. Gradually fold the dry ingredients into the creamed mixture. Fold in the white chips.

Using 2 tablespoons, drop the dough onto baking sheets in 1-inch balls, 3 inches apart. Bake in the preheated oven for 16 to 18 minutes. Let cool 10 minutes on the baking sheets, then transfer to wire racks to cool completely. Let stand 30 minutes before serving.

Chocolate Sugar Cookies

YIELD: 2 DOZEN

DOUGH

½ cup butter, softened
⅓ cup granulated sugar
1 egg
1 teaspoon pure vanilla extract
1½ cups flour
⅔ cup Ghirardelli Sweet Ground Chocolate and Cocoa
½ teaspoon baking powder
¼ teaspoon salt (optional)

GLAZE

2 tablespoons butter
½ cup Ghirardelli Sweet Ground Chocolate and Cocoa
2 to 3 tablespoons water
½ teaspoon pure vanilla extract
¾ cup confectioners' sugar

In a large mixing bowl, cream the butter and sugar until light and fluffy. Beat in the egg and vanilla extract. In a separate bowl, combine the flour, ground chocolate, baking powder, and salt; mix well. Gradually add the dry ingredients to the creamed mixture, scraping down the sides of the bowl and the beaters with a rubber spatula as needed. Cover and chill dough 1 hour.

Preheat oven to 325°. On a lightly floured surface, roll one fourth of the dough to ¼-inch thickness. (Leave the remaining dough in the refrigerator until ready to use.) With cookie cutters, cut the dough into desired shapes and place on ungreased baking sheets. Bake 5 to 7 minutes, or until no indentation remains in the cookies when pressed lightly. Cool 2 minutes on the baking sheet, then transfer to a wire rack to cool completely.

To make the glaze, melt the butter over low heat in a small, heavy saucepan. When melted, remove from the heat and add the ground chocolate and 2 tablespoons of the water, whisking continuously until mixture is smooth. Add the ½ teaspoon vanilla extract. Gradually add the confectioners' sugar, stirring with a wire whisk until smooth. Add the additional water ½ teaspoon at a time, until glaze reaches desired consistency. Drizzle or spread on cooled cookies.

Mary Pickford was performing on stage to help support her family by the age of five. She went on to become the nation's biggest box-office draw—and one of film's toughest businesswomen, negotiating the unprecedented fee of $350,000 per picture in 1917, plus veto power over directors, scripts, and co-stars. Her acting career didn't survive talkies, but she went on to found and run Mary Pickford's Cosmetics companies.

Douglas MacLean was popular in his many silent film roles and smart enough to realize that his acting career was at its end when talkies came along. He switched to producing and writing movies instead, and enjoyed a long, fruitful career.

MARY PICKFORD

MOTION PICTURE STAR
IN EVERY PACKAGE OF
GHIRARDELLI'S
MILK CHOCO[...]

DOUGLAS MacLEAN
First National Pictures

Set of Forty-Eight
Motion Picture Stars
One Card in Each Package of
Ghirardelli's Milk
Chocolate

Crunchy Turtle Cookies

YIELD: 4 DOZEN

DOUGH

1 cup sugar

⅓ cup vegetable shortening

⅓ cup butter, softened

1 teaspoon pure vanilla extract

1 egg

2 cups flour

¾ teaspoon cream of tartar

¾ teaspoon baking soda

¼ teaspoon salt (optional)

⅓ cup chopped pecans

CARAMEL LAYER

16 ounces (about 56) caramels, unwrapped

3 tablespoons heavy whipping cream

CHOCOLATE LAYER

8 ounces (2 baking bars) Ghirardelli Semi-Sweet Chocolate, broken into 1-inch pieces

1 tablespoon butter, melted

1 cup pecan halves

Preheat the oven to 350°. In a large bowl, cream the sugar, shortening, butter, vanilla extract, and egg until fluffy. In a separate bowl, combine the flour, cream of tartar, baking soda, and salt. Gradually pour the dry ingredients into the wet ingredients, mixing well. Shape the dough into 1-inch balls, and place them 3 inches apart on ungreased baking sheets. Lightly spray the bottom of a drinking glass with nonstick cooking spray, dip it in granulated sugar, and flatten one cookie into a circle approximately ¼ inch thick. Recoat the bottom of the glass with sugar and flatten another cookie. Repeat until all dough balls are flattened. Sprinkle the chopped pecans on the cookies, pressing lightly to set. Bake 9 to 10 minutes, until set but not browned.

To make the caramel layer, place the caramels and cream in a heavy saucepan and cook over low heat until melted, stirring occasionally. Spoon the caramel over the cooled cookies, to within ¼ inch of the edges.

While the caramel sets, make the chocolate layer. Melt the chocolate in a double boiler over hot, but not boiling, water. Stir occasionally until smooth. Add the melted butter, stirring until well blended. Spoon a teaspoonful of the chocolate over the caramel on each cookie; spread with the back of the spoon to cover most but not all of the caramel layer. Immediately press 1 pecan half into the chocolate on each of the cookies. Store tightly covered.

Double Chocolate-Hazelnut Biscotti

YIELD: 4 DOZEN

2 cups flour

1 cup sugar

2½ teaspoons baking powder

½ teaspoon salt

½ teaspoon baking soda

½ cup Ghirardelli Sweet Ground Chocolate and Cocoa

4 ounces (1 baking bar) Ghirardelli Semi-Sweet Chocolate, finely chopped

3 eggs

1 teaspoon pure vanilla extract

1 cup hazelnuts, coarsely chopped

Preheat the oven to 350°. Lightly grease two baking sheets.

In a large mixing bowl, whisk together the flour, sugar, baking powder, salt, baking soda, ground chocolate, and semi-sweet chocolate. In a separate bowl, combine the eggs and vanilla extract, and stir until well blended. Pour the egg mixture into the dry ingredients. Beat the mixture on medium until a dough forms (it should adhere to the beaters, approximately 2 to 3 minutes). Fold in the nuts.

Divide the dough into 4 equal parts. On the prepared baking sheets, using lightly floured hands, shape each portion into 1¼ x 10-inch logs. Place the logs at least 4 inches apart.

Bake 25 to 30 minutes. (The logs are done when they are firm to the touch.) Remove the baking sheets from the oven and let cool for 15 minutes, or until the logs are cool enough to handle.

Lower the oven temperature to 300°.

Transfer one log to a cutting board and, with a serrated knife, cut into twelve 1-inch-wide cookies. Repeat with the remaining three logs. Remove one oven rack and place the 48 cookies directly on it. Return the rack to the uppermost position in the oven and crisp 20 to 25 minutes. To test for doneness, remove one cookie; let it cool, then check it for crispness.

Transfer the cookies from the oven rack to a wire cooling rack and let cool completely. Store in a tightly covered container.

Dutch themes have often been used in Ghirardelli advertising, probably because the Dutch were famous for introducing important advances in chocolate-making. Ghirardelli has always been proud of the fact that it is one of the few American manufacturers to use a process called "dutching," after Conrad van Houten of Amsterdam, who introduced the process. Dutching helps remove acidic elements from the cocoa beans, resulting in a richer chocolate flavor and a deeper brown color.

Cocoa beans were probably first ground on stone metates like this ancient South American one from the Ghirardelli family's collection of chocolate artifacts. It is strikingly modern in design—both aesthetically and ergonomically. Note the inset front legs and slanted surface, which let a grinder kneel up close and work the stone pestle back and forth with the least possible back strain

Marbled Biscotti

YIELD: 4 DOZEN

¾ *cup Ghirardelli Semi-Sweet Chocolate Chips*
⅓ *cup butter*
¾ *cup sugar*
2 teaspoons baking powder
Pinch salt
2 eggs
½ *teaspoon pure vanilla extract*
2 cups flour
½ *cup hazelnuts, coarsely chopped*
1½ teaspoons orange zest

Preheat the oven to 350°. Lightly grease two baking sheets.

Melt the chocolate chips in a double boiler over hot, but not boiling, water. Stir the chocolate occasionally until it is smooth. Remove from the heat and cool.

In a large mixing bowl, beat the butter on medium until it is creamy, approximately 1 minute. Add the sugar, baking powder, and salt; beat until blended. Beat in the eggs and vanilla extract until combined. Stir in the flour with a wooden spoon.

Divide the dough in half and transfer one half to another bowl. Stir the melted chocolate and ¼ cup of the hazelnuts into one half of the dough. Stir the orange zest and remaining nuts into the other half. Divide each half into 4 equal parts. Using lightly floured hands, shape each portion into 1¼ x 10-inch ropes. Place a rope of each color side by side on one of the prepared baking sheets. Twist the ropes around each other several times. Flatten slightly to make a 2-inch-wide log. Repeat with the other ropes, placing the logs about 4 inches apart on the baking sheets.

Bake for 25 minutes, or until logs are firm to the touch. Cool on the baking sheets for 15 minutes, or until cool enough to handle. Lower the oven temperature to 300°.

Transfer one log to a cutting board and, with a serrated knife, cut log into twelve 1-inch-wide cookies. Repeat with the remaining three logs. Remove one oven rack and place the 48 cookies directly on it. Return the rack to the uppermost position in the oven and crisp 20 to 25 minutes. To test for doneness, remove one cookie; let it cool, then check it for crispness.

Pictured opposite page

Dipping Chocolate for Biscotti

YIELD: 1½ CUPS

1½ cups Ghirardelli Semi-Sweet Chocolate Chips
2 tablespoons vegetable shortening

Line 2 baking sheets with waxed paper. Place the chocolate in a double boiler over hot, but not boiling, water. Add the shortening and blend. Stir occasionally until the chocolate has melted. Remove the dip from the heat. Holding a cookie horizontally, dip one side of the biscotto in the mixture to cover the side and half of the top and bottom portions of the cookie. Place the biscotti chocolate-dipped side down on one of the prepared baking sheets. Repeat with remaining the biscotti. Transfer the baking sheets to a cool place and allow the chocolate to set, approximately 45 minutes to 1 hour.

White Chocolate and Almond Biscotti

Follow the recipe for Double-Chocolate Hazelnut Biscotti (see page 71), but omit the Ghirardelli Ground Sweet Chocolate and Cocoa, Ghirardelli Semi-Sweet Chocolate, hazelnuts, and pure vanilla extract. Add an additional ¼ cup flour, 4 ounces finely chopped Ghirardelli White Confection, 1 teaspoon almond extract, and 1 cup chopped or sliced natural almonds. Prepare the biscotti as the recipe directs.

Making top-quality chocolate in a highly competitive market demands the very latest, most advanced equipment. These elegant machines, shown here packing Ghirardelli's Ground Chocolate in the 1920s, were custom-designed by top European engineers. Most chocolate-making equipment still comes from Italy or Germany; with only 10 companies in the U.S. making chocolate from the bean stage through the finished product, the market for the specialized machines is too small to appeal to American suppliers.

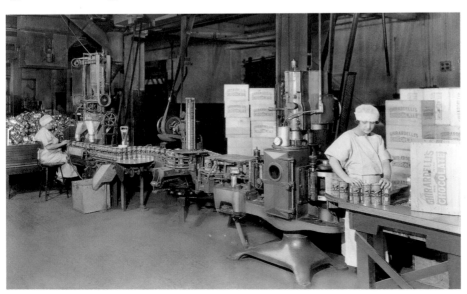

Chocolate Mint Pinwheels

YIELD: 3½ DOZEN

**4 ounces (1 baking bar) Ghirardelli Semi-Sweet Chocolate,
broken into 1-inch pieces**

½ cup butter, softened

½ cup granulated sugar

¼ cup firmly packed brown sugar

1 egg

¼ cup sour cream

2 cups flour

½ teaspoon baking powder

⅛ teaspoon baking soda

½ teaspoon salt (optional)

1 teaspoon pure vanilla extract

¼ teaspoon peppermint extract

Melt the chocolate in a double boiler over hot, but not boiling, water. Stir occasionally until the chocolate is smooth. Set aside.

In a large mixing bowl, cream the butter, granulated sugar, and brown sugar until fluffy. Add the egg and sour cream, mixing well. In a separate bowl, combine the flour, baking powder, baking soda, and salt. Gradually add the flour mixture to the large mixing bowl and mix well.

Divide the dough in half. To one half, add the melted chocolate and the vanilla extract. To the other half, add the peppermint extract. Cover both bowls of dough and chill for 1 hour.

Roll the chocolate dough between sheets of waxed paper to form a 15 x 8½-inch rectangle, ⅛ inch thick. Repeat with the peppermint dough. Place the rectangle of peppermint dough on top of the chocolate dough rectangle. Trim edges to make a neat rectangle. Roll tightly, jelly roll–style, beginning with the long side. Wrap in waxed paper and chill 1 hour.

Preheat the oven to 375°. Slice the dough roll into ¼-inch-thick slices. Place the rounds on an ungreased baking sheet. Bake 6 to 8 minutes, or until the peppermint sections of the cookies are light golden brown. Let cool for 1 minute on the baking sheet, then transfer to a wire rack to cool completely. Store covered tightly.

Chocolate-Dipped Lemon Cookies

YIELD: 5 DOZEN

DOUGH

1½ cups confectioners' sugar

1 cup butter, softened

1 egg

2 teaspoons grated lemon peel

1 teaspoon lemon extract

1 teaspoon pure vanilla extract

2½ cups flour

1 teaspoon baking powder

¼ teaspoon salt (optional)

GLAZE

12 ounces (3 baking bars) Ghirardelli Sweet Dark Chocolate, broken into 1-inch pieces

1½ tablespoons butter, melted

In a large mixing bowl, cream the confectioners' sugar and butter until fluffy. Beat in the egg, lemon peel, lemon extract, and vanilla extract. In a separate bowl, combine the flour, baking powder, and salt. Add the dry ingredients to the wet ingredients, mixing just until combined. With well-floured hands, roll the dough into a 1½-inch-wide log. Wrap the log in plastic wrap and refrigerate 30 minutes.

Preheat the oven to 350°. Slice the dough into ¼-inch-thick slices; place the rounds 1 inch apart on an ungreased baking sheet. Bake 9 to 11 minutes. Cool for 1 minute on the baking sheet, then transfer the cookies to a wire rack to cool completely.

To make the glaze, melt the chocolate in a double boiler over hot, but not boiling, water. Stir until the chocolate is smooth. Add the melted butter and continue stirring until well blended.

Line the baking sheets with waxed paper and coat lightly with nonstick cooking spray. Holding a cookie vertically, dip it halfway into the melted chocolate mixture. Place the cookie on one of the prepared baking sheets. Repeat with the remaining cookies. Transfer the baking sheets to a cool place and allow the chocolate to set, approximately 45 minutes to 1 hour. Store tightly covered with waxed paper separating layers.

Pictured opposite page (left)

Chocolate- and Apricot-Filled Triangles

YIELD: 3 DOZEN

DOUGH

1 cup butter, softened

6 ounces cream cheese, softened

⅓ cup confectioners' sugar

2⅓ cups flour

1 teaspoon grated lemon peel

1 teaspoon fresh lemon juice

FILLING

⅔ cup apricot preserves

2 ounces (½ baking bar) Ghirardelli Semi-Sweet Chocolate, chopped

GLAZE

2 ounces (½ baking bar) Ghirardelli Semi-Sweet Chocolate, broken into 1-inch pieces

½ teaspoon vegetable oil

In a small mixing bowl, beat the butter and cream cheese on medium until blended. Beat in the sugar until well combined and fluffy. Gradually add the flour, lemon peel, and lemon juice, mixing until thoroughly incorporated. Wrap dough in plastic wrap and chill 1 to 2 hours.

Combine the preserves and chocolate and set aside. Preheat the oven to 350°. Lightly grease a baking sheet.

Divide the dough into 4 equal sections. Work with one section at a time, keeping the remaining dough refrigerated. On a lightly floured surface, roll each section of the dough to form a 9-inch square, then cut each into nine 3-inch squares. Spoon 1 teaspoon of the filling onto the center of each square; brush the edges with water. Fold the squares in half diagonally and press gently with the tines of a fork to seal. Cut three small slits in the top of each. Place on the prepared baking sheet.

Bake 12 to 15 minutes, or until lightly golden brown. Cool 1 minute on the baking sheet. Transfer to a wire rack and let cool completely.

Melt the chocolate in a double boiler over hot, but not boiling, water. Blend in the vegetable oil, and stir occasionally until the chocolate is smooth. Pipe chocolate mixture (using a pastry bag) or drizzle it over the triangles in a zigzag pattern. Store loosely covered.

Note: As a variation, substitute raspberry preserves for the apricot preserves.

Pictured page 77 (right)

Peanut Butter Chocolate Cookies

YIELD: 4 DOZEN

½ cup butter, softened

½ cup creamy peanut butter

½ cup firmly packed brown sugar

¼ cup granulated sugar

1 egg

1 tablespoon milk

1 teaspoon pure vanilla extract

1 cup flour

½ teaspoon baking powder

½ teaspoon salt (optional)

1 cup Ghirardelli Semi-Sweet Chocolate Chips

¾ cup dry-roasted unsalted shelled peanuts, chopped

Preheat the oven to 350°.

In a large mixing bowl, cream the butter, peanut butter, brown sugar, and granulated sugar until well blended. Beat in the egg, milk, and vanilla. In a separate bowl, combine the flour, baking powder, and salt. Gradually add the dry ingredients to the creamed mixture. Stir in the chocolate chips and peanuts.

Drop by teaspoonfuls onto an ungreased baking sheet. Flatten with the tines of a fork to form a crisscross pattern. Bake 9 to 11 minutes, or until the edges are golden brown. Allow to cool 1 minute on the baking sheet, then transfer to a wire rack to cool completely. Store tightly covered.

Several of the artists Ghirardelli hired in the first half of this century were inspired by the Dutch motif, and created enchanting advertisements that used some variation of the little Dutch boys seen here. These ads were created at a time when Americans were less familiar with other cultures; their costumes were probably drawn from popular mythology, and not intended as a representation of the national dress.

79

Marbled Cheesecake Bars

YIELD: 16 BARS

CRUST

1 cup flour
1 cup finely chopped pecans
$\frac{1}{2}$ cup butter, softened
$\frac{1}{2}$ cup firmly packed brown sugar

BATTER

**2 ounces ($\frac{1}{2}$ baking bar) Ghirardelli Bittersweet Chocolate,
broken into 1-inch pieces**
24 ounces cream cheese, softened
$\frac{3}{4}$ cup granulated sugar
1 teaspoon pure vanilla extract
3 eggs

Preheat the oven to 325°.

To make the crust, combine the flour, pecans, butter, and brown sugar; mix well. Press the mixture onto the bottom of an ungreased 8- or 9-inch square baking pan. Bake 15 to 16 minutes, or until light golden brown. Let cool while preparing batter.

Melt the chocolate in a double boiler over hot, but not boiling, water. Stir the chocolate occasionally until smooth. Set aside.

In a large mixing bowl, beat the cream cheese, granulated sugar, and vanilla extract until well blended. Add the eggs, one at a time, mixing well after each addition. Remove 1 cup batter and reserve. Add the melted chocolate to the mixing bowl and combine. Spoon the chocolate batter over the crust. Pour the 1 cup of reserved plain batter over the chocolate batter. Using the blade of a butter knife, swirl the batter to create a marbled effect.

Bake 30 to 35 minutes, or until the center is set. Place the pan on a wire rack and cool to room temperature. Cover, and transfer the pan to the refrigerator to chill, approximately 3 hours. Store covered in the refrigerator.

Pictured opposite page

Chocolate Mexican Wedding Cookies

YIELD: 16 COOKIES

DOUGH

1 cup butter, softened
$1/3$ cup confectioners' sugar
2 teaspoons pure vanilla extract
$1^3/_4$ cups flour
1 cup ground pecans
$1/2$ cup Ghirardelli Sweet Ground Chocolate and Cocoa
$3/_4$ teaspoon ground cinnamon
Pinch salt (optional)

COATING

$1/2$ cup confectioners' sugar
$1/_4$ cup Ghirardelli Sweet Ground Chocolate and Cocoa

In a large bowl, cream the butter and confectioners' sugar until light and fluffy. Add the vanilla extract. In a separate bowl, combine the flour, ground pecans, ground chocolate, cinnamon, and salt; mix well. Gradually add the dry ingredients to the creamed mixture. Wrap dough in plastic wrap and chill 1 to 2 hours, or until firm.

Preheat the oven to 325°. Shape the dough into 1-inch balls. Place balls 1 inch apart on an ungreased baking sheet. Bake 15 to 18 minutes, or until the cookies are firm to the touch. Cool 1 minute on the baking sheet, then transfer to a wire rack.

For the coating, sift the confectioners' sugar and ground cocoa into a shallow bowl. While cookies are still warm, roll them in the coating.

Double Chocolate Brownies

YIELD: 16 TO 20 BROWNIES

2 eggs

$\frac{1}{2}$ cup sugar

1 teaspoon pure vanilla extract

$\frac{1}{2}$ cup butter, melted

1 cup Ghirardelli Sweet Ground Chocolate and Cocoa

$\frac{2}{3}$ cup flour

$\frac{1}{4}$ teaspoon baking powder

$\frac{1}{4}$ teaspoon salt

$\frac{1}{2}$ cup walnuts or pecans, coarsely chopped

$\frac{1}{2}$ cup Ghirardelli Semi-Sweet or Milk Chocolate Chips

Preheat the oven to 350°. Grease an 8-inch square pan (if not using a nonstick pan).

In a medium-sized mixing bowl, combine the eggs, sugar, and vanilla extract. Add the melted butter. In a separate bowl, sift the ground chocolate, flour, baking powder, and salt. Gradually add the dry ingredients to the egg mixture. Stir in the nuts and chocolate chips.

Spread the batter evenly into the pan. Bake 25 minutes. Place the pan on a wire rack to cool. Cut into squares and serve.

Macadamia and Coffee Chocolate Bars

YIELD: 32 BARS

1 cup butter

1 cup sugar

1 egg

$\frac{1}{4}$ cup coffee-flavored liqueur

$1\frac{3}{4}$ cups flour

6 ounces ($1\frac{1}{2}$ baking bars) Ghirardelli Bittersweet Chocolate, broken into 1-inch pieces

$3\frac{1}{2}$ ounces macadamia nuts, chopped

Preheat the oven to 350°. Grease a 15 x 10-inch jelly-roll pan.

Cream the butter and sugar until fluffy. Add the egg and liqueur, mixing well. Gradually mix in the flour. Press the dough evenly into prepared pan. Bake 25 minutes, or until golden brown. Immediately top with chocolate and allow to melt. Spread melted chocolate evenly. Sprinkle with macadamias. Place pan on wire rack and let cool to room temperature. Chill 10 minutes, or until chocolate has set. Store loosely covered.

The Ghirardelli sign is still one of the first landmarks that ship travelers see when they arrive in San Francisco, and one of the last sights they see upon leaving. At one time, the factory and ships even "talked" to each other. A brass steam whistle was blown at the factory every day to signal the beginning and end of the workday, and, as Polly Ghirardelli Lawrence recalls, "...my mother and father would be leaving on a trip on a cruise ship . . . as they would pass between here and Alcatraz, which is right opposite, this whistle would go off in a great salute, and the ship's whistle would salute back." The old whistle was discovered when the buildings were being restored in the early 1960s. Its brass gleams again, in its place of honor in the center of Ghirardelli Square.

Golden Banana Bars

YIELD: 32 BARS

1 cup firmly packed brown sugar
¾ cup butter, softened
4 medium bananas, mashed
1 egg
1 teaspoon pure vanilla extract
2 cups flour
1 cup instant or old-fashioned oatmeal, uncooked
½ teaspoon baking soda
½ teaspoon salt (optional)
1 cup Ghirardelli Semi-Sweet Chocolate Chips

Preheat the oven to 350°. In a large bowl, cream the brown sugar and butter until fluffy. Add the banana, egg, and vanilla extract. Mix well. In a separate bowl, combine the flour, oatmeal, baking soda, and salt. Gradually add the dry ingredients to the wet ingredients, mixing well. Stir in the chocolate chips.

Spread the mixture in an ungreased 9 x 13-inch baking pan. Bake 40 minutes, or until golden brown. Cool completely in the pan on a wire rack, and then cut into bars. Store loosely covered at room temperature.

Chocolate–Pecan Pie Squares

YIELD: 24 SQUARES

BASE

¾ *cup butter, softened*

1⅓ *cups granulated sugar*

3 *eggs*

1½ *cups flour*

1⅓ *cups Ghirardelli Sweet Ground Chocolate and Cocoa*

½ *teaspoon salt (optional)*

TOPPING

¼ *cup butter, melted*

2 *tablespoons flour*

¾ *cup firmly packed brown sugar*

2 *eggs*

2 *cups chopped pecans*

1 *teaspoons pure vanilla extract*

Preheat the oven to 350°. Grease the bottom only of a 9 x 13-inch pan.

In a large mixing bowl, cream the butter and granulated sugar until light and fluffy. Add the eggs, one at a time, mixing well after each addition. In a separate bowl, combine the flour, ground chocolate, and salt. Gradually add the dry ingredients to the creamed mixture, mixing until well combined. Spread the base dough into prepared pan. Set aside.

To make the topping, melt the butter over low heat in a medium-sized saucepan. Whisk in the flour, stirring until smooth. Remove pan from the heat, and add the brown sugar and eggs, mixing well. Increase the heat to medium-low, return pan to the heat, and cook 5 minutes or until thickened, stirring continuously. Remove from the heat, and stir in the pecans and vanilla extract. Spread mixture evenly over the base in pan. Bake 30 to 35 minutes, or until set. Place the pan on a wire rack and let cool completely. Store loosely covered.

This waxed paper envelope, which contained a single serving of sweetened chocolate and cocoa, dates back to an era when companies' packaging was far more simple and individually wrapped items were far less common.

Classic Blondies

YIELD: 12 TO 16 BARS

8 ounces (2 baking bars) Ghirardelli Classic White Confection, broken into 1-inch pieces

½ cup unsalted butter, cut into small pieces

2 eggs

⅓ cup sugar

1 tablespoon pure vanilla extract

1¼ cups flour

¾ teaspoon salt

1 cup Ghirardelli Semi-Sweet or Milk Chocolate Chips

Preheat the oven to 350°. Line a 9-inch square baking pan with parchment paper, then grease the paper.

Melt the white confection and butter in a double boiler over hot, but not boiling, water. Stir the mixture occasionally until smooth. Set aside.

In a large mixing bowl, beat the eggs until foamy. With the mixer running, add the sugar in a slow, steady stream. Add the vanilla extract. Add the melted confection and butter in a thin stream. By hand, fold in the flour, salt, and chocolate chips until well combined. Spoon the mixture into the prepared pan. Bake 25 minutes, or until a tester comes out clean when inserted into the center. Cut and serve warm or at room temperature. Store in an airtight container at room temperature.

Pictured opposite page

*T*his unusual billboard celebrates Ghirardelli's role at a very famous exposition—the 1939 World's Fair. The fair was held in two places that year: in New York, and in San Francisco, as the Golden Gate International Exposition. The Ghirardelli Company featured a miniature chocolate factory in its San Francisco exhibition.

Creamy Chocolate Peanut Butter Bars

YIELD: 24 BARS

CRUST

2 cups graham cracker crumbs
1/2 cup Ghirardelli Sweet Ground Chocolate and Cocoa
1/2 cup butter, melted
2 tablespoons sugar

TOPPING

16 ounces cream cheese, softened
1 cup sugar
1/2 cup creamy peanut butter
3 tablespoons flour
4 eggs
1/2 cup milk
1 teaspoon pure vanilla extract
2 ounces (1/2 baking bar) Ghirardelli Pure Milk Chocolate, broken into 1-inch pieces
1/2 teaspoon vegetable shortening

Children today find it hard to believe that candy bars once cost only a nickel or dime. But in the days of this shelf sign (above) children were lucky to get a dime for their weekly allowance. Even Polly Ghirardelli Lawrence, Domingo's great-granddaughter, only got ten cents. Of course, she probably didn't have to buy her own chocolate candy.

Preheat the oven to 350°.

To make the crust, combine the graham cracker crumbs, ground chocolate, butter, and sugar in a large mixing bowl until well blended. Press the mixture onto the bottom of an ungreased 9 x 13-inch baking pan. Bake 8 minutes, then transfer to a wire rack and let cool.

While the crust cools, make the topping. In a large bowl, beat the cream cheese, sugar, peanut butter, and flour until well blended. Add the eggs, one at a time, mixing well after each addition. Blend in the milk and the vanilla extract. Pour the filling into the crust and bake 40 minutes, or until just set. Place pan on wire rack and let cool completely.

Melt the chocolate pieces and vegetable shortening in a double boiler over hot, but not boiling, water. Stir occasionally until smooth. Spread the melted chocolate evenly over the cooled bars. Chill approximately 10 minutes, just until the chocolate layer is partially set. Score the chocolate layer with a sharp knife, forming squares, and return the pan to the refrigerator. Chill 30 minutes, or until firm. Cut through the bars and serve. Store tightly covered in the refrigerator.

Pictured opposite page

Breads
and
Pastries

Buttermilk Scones with Milk Chocolate Chips

YIELD: 12 SCONES

2 cups flour

1 tablespoon baking powder

½ teaspoon baking soda

½ teaspoon salt

½ cup confectioners' sugar

6 tablespoons butter, chilled and cut into 12 pieces

2 eggs

⅓ cup buttermilk

1 tablespoon pure vanilla extract

¾ cup Ghirardelli Milk Chocolate Chips

Preheat the oven to 425°. Lightly grease a baking sheet or line with parchment paper.

In a large bowl, sift together the flour, baking powder, baking soda, salt, and confectioners' sugar. Add the butter and cut it into the dry ingredients until the mixture resembles coarse crumbs. In a small bowl, lightly beat the eggs, then add the buttermilk and vanilla extract. Stir until combined. Add half of the buttermilk mixture to the dry ingredients and gently fold in until almost combined. Add the chocolate chips and the remaining buttermilk mixture to the batter and stir until just incorporated and still lumpy. (Do not overmix or the scones will be tough.)

Drop the scones in ¼-cup portions onto the prepared baking sheet. Bake 12 minutes, or until golden brown. Let the scones cool on the baking sheet 5 minutes before transferring them to a wire rack. Serve warm or at room temperature. Scones will last for 1 to 2 days at room temperature. The scones freeze well in an airtight container.

Note: Sour milk may be substituted for buttermilk. To make sour milk, place 2 teaspoons vinegar or lemon juice in a measuring cup, and add enough milk to measure ⅓ cup. Stir and let stand 5 minutes.

Pictured opposite page (right)

YOU CAN
ACCOMPLISH
WONDERS
with chocolate if you use

Ghirardelli's
the original
GROUND
CHOCOLATE

White Chocolate–Raspberry Muffins

YIELD: 12 MUFFINS

¼ cup butter

½ cup plus 1 tablespoon sugar

1 egg

1 cup milk

1 teaspoon pure vanilla extract

1 tablespoon baking powder

2 cups plus 1 tablespoon flour

8 ounces (2 baking bars) Ghirardelli White Confection, finely chopped

½ cup fresh raspberries

Preheat the oven to 400°. Grease 12 medium-sized muffin cups or line with paper baking cups.

In a medium-sized bowl, cream the butter and sugar until smooth. Add the egg, milk, and vanilla extract and stir until combined. In a large bowl, place the baking powder, 2 cups of the flour, and the white confection, and whisk to combine. Gradually add to the creamed mixture, mixing just until combined. Add the raspberries, and stir just until they are incorporated. (The batter will be slightly lumpy.)

Fill the prepared muffin cups three-quarters full. In a small bowl, add the remaining 1 tablespoon of sugar and flour, and mix well to thoroughly combine. Dust the muffins with the sugar mixture. Bake 20 to 25 minutes, or until the center of a muffin springs back when pressed lightly. Cool the muffins in the pan on a wire rack 5 minutes, then carefully remove them and serve warm, or transfer muffins to the wire rack to cool completely before serving. Store in an airtight container at room temperature; to refresh, heat 5 minutes in 425° oven.

Pictured page 93 (left)

White Chocolate and Almond Coffee Cake

YIELD: 12 TO 16 SERVINGS

BATTER

1½ cups granulated sugar

3 eggs

1 cup butter, softened

1½ teaspoons almond extract

1½ teaspoons baking powder

1½ teaspoons baking soda

2¼ cups flour

1 cup sour cream

4 ounces (1 baking bar) Ghirardelli Classic White Confection,
finely chopped

FILLING

¼ cup light brown sugar

½ cup Ghirardelli Classic White Chips

½ cup chopped almonds

2 tablespoons confectioners' sugar

Preheat the oven to 350°. Lightly grease a 12-cup bundt pan.

In a large mixing bowl, beat the granulated sugar, eggs, and butter on low until fluffy. Add the almond extract, baking powder, baking soda, flour, sour cream, and chopped white confection. Continue beating until blended. Spoon half the batter into the prepared pan.

To prepare the filling, combine the brown sugar, white chips, and almonds, mixing well. Carefully spread the filling over the batter. Spoon the remaining batter over the filling.

Bake 1 hour to 1 hour 10 minutes, or until golden brown and a tester comes out clean when inserted into the center of the cake. Set the pan on a rack to cool for 15 minutes, then invert the cake onto a serving plate. Sift the confectioners' sugar over the top of the cake. Serve warm or at room temperature.

Chocolate Gingerbread

YIELD: 16 SERVINGS

BATTER

¾ cup butter, softened

1 cup granulated sugar

3 eggs

⅓ cup molasses

3 cups flour

¾ cup Ghirardelli Sweet Ground Chocolate and Cocoa

1 teaspoon baking powder

1 teaspoon baking soda

1 teaspoon ground cinnamon

1 teaspoon ground ginger

1 teaspoon salt (optional)

1 cup buttermilk

TOPPING

1 cup heavy whipping cream

3 tablespoons confectioners' sugar

1 tablespoon Ghirardelli Sweet Ground Chocolate and Cocoa

½ teaspoon pure vanilla extract

Preheat the oven to 350°. Grease a 9 x 13-inch baking pan. Cream the butter and sugar until light and fluffy. Beat in the eggs, one at a time, mixing well after each addition. Beat in the molasses. In a separate bowl, combine the flour, ground chocolate, baking powder, baking soda, cinnamon, ginger, and salt. Alternatively, add the dry ingredients and buttermilk to the creamed mixture, beating well and scraping down the sides of the bowl and the beaters with a rubber spatula after each addition. Spread batter in the prepared pan. Bake 40 to 45 minutes, or until a tester comes out clean when inserted into the center of the gingerbread. Place pan on a wire rack and let cool completely.

To make the topping, beat the whipping cream until soft peaks form. In a separate bowl, combine the confectioners' sugar, ground chocolate, and vanilla extract. Gradually add the confectioner's sugar mixture to the cream and continue beating until stiff peaks form.

Cut gingerbread into squares and serve with a dollop of topping.

Note: Sour milk may be substituted for buttermilk. To make sour milk, place 3 teaspoons vinegar or lemon juice in a measuring cup, and add enough milk to measure 1 cup. Stir and let stand 5 minutes.

Chocolate Banana-Nut Bread

YIELD: TWO 9-INCH LOAVES

¾ cup butter, softened

2 cups sugar

4 eggs

½ cup milk

4 large bananas, mashed

3½ cups flour

1 cup Ghirardelli Sweet Ground Chocolate and Cocoa

1 tablespoon plus 2 teaspoons baking powder

1 teaspoon salt

1½ cups hazelnuts, chopped

Preheat the oven to 350°. Lightly grease two 9 x 5-inch loaf pans.

In a large bowl, cream the butter and sugar until fluffy. Beat in the eggs, adding one at a time, mixing well after each addition. Add the milk and bananas, beating until well blended. In a separate bowl, whisk together the flour, ground chocolate, baking powder, and salt. Gradually, add the dry ingredients to the creamed mixture. Mix on low only until evenly combined. Stir in the nuts. (Do not overmix.)

Pour batter into the prepared pans. Bake 1 hour to 1 hour 15 minutes, or until golden brown and a tester comes out clean when inserted into the center of the bread. Set the pans on a rack to cool for 15 minutes, then turn the loaves out of the pans to cool completely.

Good manufacturing practices have always been important in chocolate-making. These gleaming machines of the 1930s are clearly old-fashioned, but their capped and gowned operators look much like Ghirardelli's workers today. Proper handling is essential, not only because chocolate is a food product, but because it is one of the most vulnerable to environmental factors. Ventilation is crucial, as well: excess moisture can cloud glossy finishes, and chocolate picks up stray odors so readily that a worker's strong perfume could taint an entire batch.

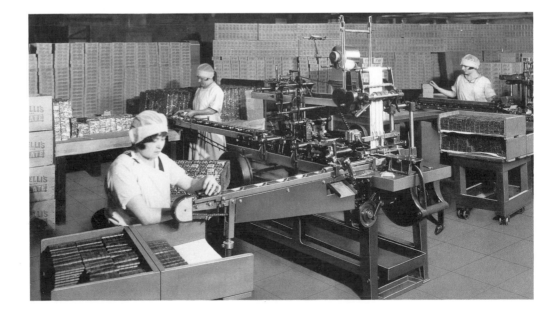

Lemon Chocolate Chip Bread

YIELD: TWO 9-INCH LOAVES

¾ cup butter, softened

1½ cups granulated sugar

4 eggs

2 cups milk

1 teaspoon salt

4 teaspoons baking powder

3 cups flour

2 3.4-ounce packages instant lemon pudding and pie filling

1¼ cups Ghirardelli Semi-Sweet Chocolate Chips,
coarsely chopped

¼ cup confectioners' sugar

These postcards were a delightful and effective way to promote Ghirardelli's hot cocoa as a favorite drink that families and friends would share through the generations. The "cocoa party" illustration is so charming it has been revived on a contemporary Ghirardelli gift.

Preheat the oven to 350°. Lightly grease two 9 x 5-inch loaf pans.

In a large mixing bowl, cream the butter and granulated sugar. Add the eggs and milk, and blend well. In another bowl, whisk the salt, baking powder, flour, and pie filling mix.

Add the dry ingredients to the liquid ingredients. Beat on medium for 2 minutes. (The batter will be thick.) Allow the batter to stand 5 minutes.

Add the chocolate chips and gently stir. Pour the batter into the prepared loaf pans. Bake 1 hour, or until golden brown and a tester comes out clean when inserted into the center of a loaf. Let the pans cool on a wire rack for 15 minutes before turning the loaves out of the pans and transferring them to the rack to cool completely. Dust with the confectioners' sugar. To store, wrap tightly in aluminum foil and keep at room temperature for up to 3 days or freeze.

Pictured opposite page

Chocolate-Orange Muffins

YIELD: 12 MUFFINS

TOPPING

$\frac{1}{3}$ *cup flour*

3 tablespoons sugar

$\frac{1}{2}$ *teaspoon grated orange peel*

3 tablespoons butter

BATTER

1$\frac{1}{4}$ cups flour

$\frac{2}{3}$ *cup Ghirardelli Sweet Ground Chocolate and Cocoa*

$\frac{1}{4}$ *cup sugar*

1$\frac{1}{2}$ teaspoons baking powder

$\frac{1}{2}$ *teaspoon baking soda*

$\frac{1}{4}$ *teaspoon salt (optional)*

$\frac{3}{4}$ *cup milk*

$\frac{1}{3}$ *cup butter, melted*

1 egg

$\frac{1}{2}$ *teaspoon grated orange peel*

*4 ounces (1 baking bar) Ghirardelli Sweet Dark Chocolate,
finely chopped*

To make the topping, combine the flour, sugar, and orange peel; mix well. Cut in the butter until the mixture resembles coarse crumbs. Set aside.

Preheat the oven to 400°. Grease 12 medium-sized muffin cups or line with paper baking cups.

In a large mixing bowl, combine the flour, ground chocolate, sugar, baking powder, baking soda, and salt; mix well. In a separate bowl, combine the milk, butter, egg, and orange peel. Add the milk mixture to the dry ingredients and mix just until dry ingredients are moistened. Fold in the chopped chocolate.

Fill the prepared muffin cups three-quarters full. Sprinkle with topping. Bake 15 to 18 minutes, or until the center springs back when pressed lightly. Place pan on wire rack and cool 5 minutes, then serve.

Double Chocolate Cupcakes

YIELD: 12 CUPCAKES

4 ounces cream cheese, softened

⅓ cup plus ½ cup sugar

1 egg

4 ounces (1 baking bar) Ghirardelli Semi-Sweet Chocolate,
finely chopped

1 cup flour

3 tablespoons Ghirardelli Unsweetened Premium Cocoa

½ teaspoon baking soda

½ cup water

3 tablespoons vegetable oil

2 teaspoons white vinegar

1 teaspoon pure vanilla extract

⅓ cup slivered blanched almonds, chopped

Preheat the oven to 350°. Grease 12 medium-sized muffin cups or line with paper baking cups.

In a small mixing bowl, combine the cream cheese and ⅓ cup of the sugar, beating until well blended. Beat in the egg. Stir in the semi-sweet chocolate. Set aside.

In a medium-sized mixing bowl, combine the flour, the remaining ½ cup of sugar, the cocoa, and the baking soda. In a small mixing bowl, combine the water, oil, vinegar, and vanilla extract, mixing until well blended. Fill each prepared muffin cup one-third full. Top each cup with 1 tablespoon of the chocolate-cream cheese mixture. Sprinkle with almonds. Bake 18 to 20 minutes.

Cool muffins in the pan on a wire rack 5 minutes. Carefully remove the cupcakes from the pan and transfer them to the rack to cool completely.

These women are packing milk chocolate bars around 1943, so the bars are probably headed for armed service ration packs. Millions of Ghirardelli chocolate bars helped sustain American military forces through both world wars. It's easy to imagine the comfort they brought to homesick soldiers.

Supplies of sugar and cocoa beans were hard to import during WWII, and chocolate was rationed on the home front. But some cocoa was available, and Ghirardelli helped the war effort by designing packaging that saved precious metal.

Chocolate Cinnamon Buns

YIELD: 12 BUNS

1 envelope active dry yeast

$\frac{1}{4}$ cup plus 2 tablespoons granulated sugar

$\frac{3}{4}$ cup warm water

$\frac{1}{4}$ cup vegetable shortening

$\frac{1}{4}$ teaspoon salt

1 egg

$\frac{1}{4}$ cup plus 2 tablespoons Ghirardelli Unsweetened Premium Cocoa

2 cups and 2 tablespoons sifted flour

1 tablespoon butter, softened

$1\frac{1}{4}$ teaspoons ground cinnamon

1 cup sifted confectioners' sugar

2 tablespoons milk

$\frac{1}{3}$ cup chopped walnuts

Grease a 9-inch square baking pan.

In a small bowl, dissolve the yeast and 1 tablespoon of the granulated sugar in the warm water. In a large mixing bowl, combine the shortening, salt, 3 tablespoons of the granulated sugar, the egg, cocoa, and 1 cup of the flour. Add the yeast mixture and beat until smooth. Stir in the remaining 1 cup and 2 tablespoons of flour to form a stiff dough.

Place the dough in a well-greased bowl. Cover the bowl with plastic wrap and let it rise in a warm place (80 to 85 degrees) for approximately 1 hour and 30 minutes, or until the dough has doubled in size.

Punch the dough down. On a lightly floured surface, roll the dough into a 14 x 9-inch rectangle. Spread with the butter.

In a small bowl, combine the remaining 2 tablespoons of sugar and the cinnamon; sprinkle the mixture over the dough. Loosely roll up jelly roll-style. Moisten the edges with water and press together to seal. Cut the rolls into 1-inch-wide slices. Place the slices in the prepared pan. Cover with a kitchen towel and let rise 1 hour, or until doubled in size.

Preheat the oven to 375°.

Bake 25 minutes. Combine the confectioners' sugar and milk, mixing until well combined. Spoon the glaze over the warm rolls. Sprinkle the walnuts over the glaze.

Pictured opposite page

Chocolate Zucchini Bread

YIELD: ONE 9-INCH LOAF

1¼ cups sugar

1 cup vegetable oil

½ cup water

2 eggs

1½ teaspoons pure vanilla extract

3 cups flour

½ teaspoon ground cinnamon

½ teaspoon salt (optional)

½ teaspoon baking soda

¼ teaspoon baking powder

1¼ cups shredded zucchini

8 ounces (2 baking bars) Ghirardelli Milk Chocolate, broken into ¼-inch pieces

Preheat the oven to 350°. Grease a 9 x 5-inch pan.

In a large bowl, combine the sugar, oil, water, eggs, and vanilla extract. Mix until well blended. In a separate bowl, combine the flour, cinnamon, salt, baking soda, and baking powder. Gradually add the dry ingredients to the wet ingredients, stirring just until the dry ingredients are moistened. Stir in the zucchini and chocolate pieces. Spoon the batter into the prepared pan, spreading it evenly. Bake 1 hour 20 minutes to 1 hour 30 minutes, or until a tester comes out clean when inserted into the center of the loaf. Cool the bread in the pan on a wire rack for 15 minutes, then transfer to a wire rack to cool completely. To store, wrap tightly in aluminum foil and keep at room temperature for up to 3 days or freeze.

Confections and Other Desserts

Classic Fudge

YIELD: 16 SQUARES

2 cups Ghirardelli Semi-Sweet Chocolate Chips

**2 ounces (½ baking bar) Ghirardelli Unsweetened Chocolate,
cut into ½-inch pieces**

14 ounces canned sweetened condensed milk

2½ teaspoons pure vanilla extract

1 cup chopped walnuts

Line an 8-inch square baking pan with waxed paper.

Place chocolate chips, unsweetened chocolate, and the sweetened condensed milk in a double boiler over hot, but not boiling, water. Stir the mixture occasionally until the chocolate has melted. Stir in the vanilla extract and nuts. Spread fudge evenly in the prepared baking pan. Refrigerate for 2 hours, or until firm. Cut when cool and firm. Store, uncovered, in the refrigerator.

Pictured opposite page (left)

English Toffee

YIELD: 1¼ POUNDS

¾ cup pecans, finely chopped

1 cup butter

1 cup sugar

2 tablespoons water

⅛ teaspoon salt (optional)

1 teaspoon pure vanilla extract

**8 ounces (2 baking bars) Ghirardelli Bittersweet Chocolate,
broken into 1-inch pieces**

Preheat the oven to 350°. Toast the chopped pecans on a baking sheet in the oven for 6 to 8 minutes, or until fragrant. With heavy-duty aluminum foil, form a 10-inch-square shell with 1-inch-high sides. Place the foil shell on a baking sheet and set aside.

In a heavy saucepan, cook the butter, sugar, water, and salt over medium heat until the temperature reaches 305° (hard-crack stage), stirring occasionally. (Watch closely after it reaches 290° because the temperature will increase rapidly.) When the mixture becomes dark golden brown, immediately remove the pan from the heat. Stir in the vanilla extract. Pour the mixture into the foil shell. It will spread but may not reach the edges of the square. Cool at room temperature for 45 minutes, or until hard.

Melt the chocolate in a double boiler over hot, but not boiling, water. Stir occasionally until the chocolate is smooth. Immediately spread melted chocolate over the cooled toffee and sprinkle with the pecans, pressing lightly to set pecans into chocolate. Let set at room temperature 1 hour, or until the chocolate is set. Break toffee into pieces. Store covered at room temperature for up to 1 month.

Pictured opposite page (right)

Pecan and Caramel Chocolate Clusters

YIELD: 24 PIECES

1 cup pecan halves

1 cup sugar

1 cup dark corn syrup

1 cup butter

1 cup heavy whipping cream

6 ounces (1½ baking bars) Ghirardelli Pure Milk Chocolate, broken into 1-inch pieces

Line a baking sheet with waxed paper or spray it with nonstick cooking spray.

Cut the pecan halves in half lengthwise and arrange them to form 24 circles approximately 1½ inches in diameter on the prepared baking sheet.

In a 3-quart heavy saucepan, cook the sugar, dark corn syrup, butter, and ½ cup of the cream, stirring occasionally, over low heat, until the sugar has dissolved. Increase the heat to medium and stir continuously until the temperature reaches 240° on a candy thermometer. Remove the pan from the heat and stir in the remaining cream. Return the pan to the heat and cook until the temperature reaches 245°, stirring continuously.

Line a 9-inch square baking pan with aluminum foil. Pour the caramel into the pan and let it cool approximately 2 minutes. Spoon approximately 1 tablespoon of the caramel over each circle of pecans.

Melt the chocolate in a double boiler over hot, but not boiling water. Remove the chocolate form the heat and spread it over the caramel on each cluster. Chill 10 minutes, then let stand at room temperature until the chocolate is firm. Store tightly covered at room temperature.

*T*he Clock Tower, the highest point of Ghirardelli Square, once housed the offices of chocolate executives. The elegant dormered tower gives a lift to the profile of the Square and lends the Victorian grace that is so characteristic of San Francisco architecture. This etching shows, even better than photographs can, how beautifully the original Ghirardelli architect William Mooser combined brick, white stone, and wood to achieve imposing size without heaviness.

Silky Chocolate Mousse

YIELD: 6 SERVINGS

3 cups heavy whipping cream

½ cup sugar

1 cup water

2 cups Ghirardelli Semi-Sweet Chocolate Chips

6 egg yolks

Chill a medium-large mixing bowl and beaters.

Pour cream into chilled bowl and whip until stiff peaks form. Set aside. In a saucepan, bring the sugar and water to a boil and continue boiling for 3 minutes. Pour the sugar mixture into a blender and add the chocolate chips. Blend on low for 20 seconds. Add the egg yolks and blend 15 seconds more. Carefully pour the chocolate mixture into the bowl of whipped cream, being careful not the deflate it, and fold it in until smooth.

Transfer the mousse to an airtight container and freeze overnight or at least 12 hours. To serve, defrost, stir until smooth, and spoon into serving glasses.

Note: This mousse must be frozen and thawed for best results. Never serve it the day you make it.

Sweet Ground Chocolate with Cocoa has been the Ghirardelli flagship product for over a century. It's unlike any other cocoa drink product on grocery shelves because it not only contains cocoa, sugar, and vanilla, but it also has extra chocolate liquor—the pure, ground chocolate essence of cocoa beans, to deliver a richer chocolate taste than cocoa alone.

Some companies tout their "breakfast cocoa"; but this only means they meet the minimum industry standards for cocoa butter content of at least 22 percent. All modern Ghirardelli cocoas contain 22 to 24 percent cocoa butter—the highest percentage that cocoa can have and still blend with liquids.

Ghirardelli no longer markets an "instant" chocolate drink and will not, until company researchers discover how to make one that has the richness of a milk-based drink and that can be made by adding just hot water. Currently, "instant" products contain dry milk solids, which are disappointing to those who are used to old-fashioned milk-based hot chocolates.

Sinful Chocolate Truffles

YIELD: 30 TRUFFLES

¼ cup heavy whipping cream

8 ounces (2 baking bars) Ghirardelli Bittersweet Chocolate, broken into ¼-inch pieces

6 tablespoons unsalted butter, cut into small pieces

⅓ cup Ghirardelli Unsweetened Premium Cocoa

In a small saucepan, bring the cream to a simmer. Remove from the heat, and stir in the chocolate and butter. In a medium-sized skillet, bring ½ inch water to a slow simmer. Set the saucepan in the skillet over low heat. Stir mixture just until chocolate has completely melted. Remove from the heat.

Pour the chocolate mixture into a shallow bowl. Cool, cover, and refrigerate until firm, at least 2 hours.

Pour the cocoa into a pie plate. Line an airtight container with waxed paper. Dip a melon baller or small spoon into a glass of warm water and quickly scrape across the surface of the chilled truffle mixture to form a rough 1-inch ball. Drop the ball into the cocoa. Repeat with the remaining truffle mixture.

Gently shake the pie plate to coat truffles evenly. Transfer truffles to the prepared container, separating layers with additional waxed paper. Cover tightly and refrigerate up to 2 weeks, or freeze up to 3 months.

Pictured opposite page

Dipping Chocolate for Truffles

10 ounces (2½ baking bars) Ghirardelli Bittersweet Chocolate, broken into ¼-inch pieces

Line a baking sheet with waxed paper. Form the truffles and place on the prepared baking sheet. (Do not coat in cocoa.) Freeze, uncovered, at least 2 hours.

Melt the chocolate in a double boiler over hot, but not boiling, water. Stir the chocolate occasionally until smooth. Remove the truffles from the freezer. Drop one ball into the melted chocolate. Twirl briefly with a fork to coat. Lift the truffle with the fork and drain over the saucepan; return to the baking sheet. Repeat with the remaining truffles. Place the baking sheet in the refrigerator and allow the chocolate coating to set, approximately 1 hour. Place truffles in a waxed paper-lined airtight container. Store up to 2 weeks in the refrigerator or up to 3 months in the freezer.

White Crème Brûlée

YIELD: 4 SERVINGS

4 egg yolks

¹/₃ cup plus 4 teaspoons sugar

2 cups heavy whipping cream

*4 ounces (1 baking bar) Ghirardelli Classic White Confection,
broken into ¹/₄-inch pieces*

¹/₂ teaspoon pure vanilla extract

12 raspberries, for garnish

4 sprigs fresh mint, for garnish

Preheat the oven to 300°.

In a medium-sized bowl, whisk the egg yolks and ¹/₃ cup of the sugar until smooth. In a 2-quart saucepan, bring the whipping cream to a simmer over medium-high heat, stirring continuously. Add the white confection to the cream. Remove the saucepan from the heat and whisk the mixture until the white confection has melted. Gradually add to the egg yolk mixture, whisking continuously until smooth. Add the vanilla extract.

Pour the mixture into four ramekins or custard cups. Place the ramekins in a 9 x 13-inch baking pan. Pour water into the pan (do not allow any water to fall into the ramekins) until the ramekins are sitting in 1 to 1¹/₂ inches of water.

Bake 45 minutes, or until set. Gently jiggle the ramekins to determine whether the crème brûlée is done; the centers should wiggle just slightly. Remove from the oven, preheat the broiler, and sprinkle 1 teaspoon of the remaining sugar over each ramekin. Return to the oven and place under the broiler until sugar has caramelized. Garnish each ramekin with 3 raspberries and 1 mint sprig, and serve chilled. The crème brûlée may be covered and stored in the refrigerator overnight.

Pictured opposite page

In 1852, the year that Domingo Ghirardelli established his chocolate company in San Francisco, an English recipe book, *Cookery Book for the Working Classes,* published this recipe for making a hot drink of chocolate "nibs" (roasted but unground cocoa beans):

> Boil gently two ounces of cocoa nibs in three pints of water for two hours and a half; without allowing it to reduce more than one-third; that is, the three pints should be boiled down to one quart. When sufficiently boiled, strain the cocoa from the nibs, mix it with equal proportions of milk, and sweeten with sugar. . . sufficient cocoa for the breakfasts of four persons. This would be much wholesomer and cheaper than tea. To be sure, it would take some trouble and care to prepare it, and this should be attended to over-night.

Evidently people of modest means were willing to go to considerable trouble to enjoy a chocolate drink. Powdered cocoa was available at the time, but it was more expensive. Advertisements in the front of the *Cookery Book* included one for "Epp's Cocoa (Commonly called Epp's Homeopathic Cocoa), Distinguished for its Delicious Aroma, Grateful Smoothness, and Invigorating Power."

Hot Chocolate Soufflé

YIELD: 8 SERVINGS

¼ cup plus 2 tablespoons granulated sugar

6 ounces (1½ baking bars) Ghirardelli Semi-Sweet Chocolate, broken into 1-inch pieces

1 tablespoon flour

½ cup heavy whipping cream or half-and-half

4 eggs, separated

½ teaspoon pure vanilla extract

Pinch salt (optional)

Pinch cream of tartar

2 teaspoons confectioners' sugar

Preheat the oven to 375°. Butter a 1½-quart ceramic soufflé dish. Sprinkle the inside of the dish with 2 tablespoons of the granulated sugar to coat.

Melt the chocolate in a double boiler over hot, but not boiling, water. Stir the chocolate occasionally until smooth.

In a medium-sized heavy saucepan, combine the remaining granulated sugar and the flour and mix well. Add the whipping cream. Cook over medium heat until the sugar melts. Beat egg yolks. Gradually add a small amount of the warm sugar-cream mixture to the egg yolks, stirring continuously. Pour the egg mixture into the saucepan and mix well.

Remove the saucepan from the heat. Stir in the melted chocolate, vanilla extract, and salt. Set aside to cool. In a large bowl, beat the egg whites with the cream of tartar until stiff peaks form. Gently fold the cooled chocolate mixture into the egg whites until no streaks of white remain. Spoon the soufflé into the prepared dish.

Bake 30 to 35 minutes, or until puffed. Dust with the confectioners' sugar. Serve immediately.

Note: If desired, serve the souffle with Amaretto Chocolate Sauce (page 128) or Chocolate–De Menthe Sauce (page 130).

Creamy White Chocolate Pudding with Strawberries

YIELD: 4 SERVINGS

2 tablespoons plus 1 teaspoon cornstarch

2 tablespoons sugar

2 cups milk

10 ounces (2½ baking bars) Ghirardelli Classic White Confection, finely chopped

1 teaspoon pure vanilla extract

10 ounces frozen strawberries in syrup, thawed

12 fresh whole strawberries, for garnish

In a small bowl, combine the cornstarch, sugar, and ¾ cup of the milk.

In a medium-sized saucepan, bring the remaining 1¼ cups of milk to a simmer. Gradually stir ½ cup of the hot milk into the cornstarch mixture. Return the cornstarch-milk mixture to the saucepan and cook until the pudding thickens, approximately 10 minutes.

Add the white confection to the pudding mixture, and stir until blended. Allow the pudding to cool slightly, then add the vanilla extract and stir gently.

Pour the pudding into four ramekins or small bowls. Cover, and refrigerate at least 2 hours.

Place the thawed strawberries in a blender and blend until smooth. Serve the pudding with the strawberry sauce and garnish with fresh strawberries.

GHIRARDELLI'S
Ground Chocolate

Tiramisu

YIELD: 15 SERVINGS

12 ounces mascarpone cheese

½ cup plus 1 tablespoon Ghirardelli Sweet Ground Chocolate and Cocoa

⅓ cup confectioners' sugar

½ cup coffee-flavored liqueur

1½ teaspoons pure vanilla extract

½ teaspoon salt (optional)

1½ cups heavy whipping cream

2 tablespoons water

2 teaspoons powdered instant espresso coffee

6 ounces ladyfingers (about 2 dozen), halved

In a large mixing bowl, beat the mascarpone, 6 tablespoons of the ground chocolate, ¼ cup of the confectioners' sugar, ¼ cup of the liqueur, 1 teaspoon of the vanilla extract, and the salt with a wire whisk. Set aside.

In a small bowl beat 1 cup of the whipping cream until stiff peaks form. Fold the whipped cream into the mascarpone mixture.

In another small bowl, combine the remaining ¼ cup liqueur, the remaining ½ teaspoon of vanilla extract, the water, and the espresso powder. Line a 2½-quart glass or crystal bowl with one fourth of the ladyfingers; brush with 2 tablespoons of the espresso mixture. Spoon one third of the mascarpone mixture over the ladyfingers. Repeat, making 2 more layers of ladyfingers brushed with the espresso mixture and topped with the mascarpone mixture. Top with the remaining ladyfingers, gently pressing them into the cheese mixture. Brush the ladyfingers with the remaining espresso mixture. Sprinkle 1 tablespoon of ground chocolate over the top.

In a small mixing bowl, beat the remaining ½ cup whipping cream and the remaining confectioners' sugar until stiff peaks form. Spoon the whipped cream into a decorating bag with a large star-shaped tip. Pipe large rosettes on top of the dessert. Sprinkle the remaining 2 tablespoons of ground chocolate on the rosettes. Chill at least 2 hours.

Note: If you cannot find mascarpone cheese, substitute 16 ounces of softened cream cheese and 3 tablespoons of milk. Beat on medium until smooth and fluffy. Add 6 tablespoons of the ground chocolate, ½ cup confectioners' sugar, 3 tablespoons coffee-flavored liqueur, 1 teaspoon pure vanilla extract, and omit the salt; set aside. Continue as the recipe directs.

Pictured opposite page

Chocolate-Drizzled Baklava

YIELD: 16 SERVINGS

8 ounces (2 baking bars) Ghirardelli Bittersweet Chocolate

3 cups finely chopped walnuts

½ cup sugar

1 teaspoon ground cinnamon

16 ounces frozen phyllo dough, thawed and covered with a damp towel

1 cup butter, melted

1 cup honey

Preheat the oven to 300°.

Finely chop 7 ounces of the chocolate. Set aside remaining chocolate (for the topping).

Combine the chopped chocolate, walnuts, sugar, and cinnamon. Divide into 4 equal portions, about 1 cup each. Set aside.

Lightly butter a 9 x 13-inch glass baking dish. Cut the phyllo dough into 9 x 13-inch rectangles, keeping the dough covered with a damp cloth while working to prevent it from drying. Place 1 phyllo sheet in the dish and brush the top with melted butter. Repeat layering and buttering 7 times. Sprinkle 1 cup of the walnut mixture over the first 8 layers. Repeat 3 more times, ending with the walnut mixture. Top with the remaining phyllo sheets.

With a sharp knife, make 2 cuts lengthwise in the phyllo, taking care to cut only the top layers of dough. Then make 8 diagonal cuts to form diamond-shaped pieces. Brush the top with the remaining butter.

Bake 1 hour 15 minutes, or until the top is golden brown. Meanwhile, heat the honey until warm. Pour over the hot baklava. Cool on a wire rack for 1 hour, then cover with aluminum foil and let stand at room temperature until ready to serve.

When ready to serve, melt the remaining 1 ounce of chocolate in a double boiler over hot, but not boiling, water. Stir occasionally until the chocolate is smooth. To serve, cut completely through all layers. Using a spoon or pastry bag (see page 20) drizzle the baklava with the melted chocolate.

Pictured opposite page

The candy bar is one of the most popular forms of chocolate. Candy bars are not only convenient, but they also allow Ghirardelli respond to changing tastes by adding elements that mirror the tastes of the times. With the new interest in seeds and grains in the late 1970s, for instance, Ghirardelli featured granola and sesame seed bars. The company's latest offerings include a Double Chocolate Mocha Bar and a White Chocolate Mocha & Biscotti Bar, both imbedded with tiny, crisp cookie bits, reflecting the current popularity of coffee and coffee houses.

Double-Dipped Chocolate Strawberries

YIELD: 2 DOZEN

8 ounces (2 baking bars) Ghirardelli Bittersweet Chocolate, broken into 1-inch pieces

1 pint (about 24 medium) whole strawberries, washed, dried, and at room temperature

4 ounces (1 baking bar) Ghirardelli Pure Milk Chocolate, broken into 1-inch pieces

Melt the bittersweet chocolate in a double boiler over hot, but not boiling, water. Line a baking sheet with waxed paper.

Hold one strawberry by the stem and dip it almost to the top in the melted bittersweet chocolate; let the excess drip off. Transfer the strawberry to the prepared baking sheet. Repeat with the remaining strawberries. Chill until the chocolate has set, approximately 15 minutes.

Melt the milk chocolate in a double boiler over hot, but not boiling, water. Again, hold one strawberry by the stem, and dip it halfway into the milk chocolate; let the excess drip off. Return the double-dipped strawberry to the baking sheet and repeat with the remaining strawberries. Chill until the chocolate has set, approximately 15 minutes. Let stand at room temperature at least 30 minutes before serving.

Note: Dip strawberries quickly, because the chocolate will become too thick to use for dipping within 10 minutes after it has melted.

Irresistible Chocolate Malt

YIELD: TWO 8-OUNCE MALTS

1 cup vanilla ice cream

¾ cup milk

2 tablespoons Ghirardelli Sweet Ground Chocolate and Cocoa

1 tablespoon malted milk powder

2 tablespoons Sweetened Whipped Cream (page 60), for garnish

Place two 10-ounce parfait glasses in the freezer to chill.

In a blender, combine the ice cream, milk, ground chocolate, and malted milk powder and blend until well mixed. Pour half of the malt mixture into each of the chilled glasses and garnish with the whipped cream. Serve immediately.

Chocolate Mint Malt

Follow the recipe for the Irresistible Chocolate Malt, but add ¼ teaspoon mint extract to the malt ingredients and blend. Garnish with fresh mint leaves.

Chocolate Banana Malt

Follow the recipe for the Irresistible Chocolate Malt, but add ½ medium banana to the malt ingredients and blend. Garnish with a slice of banana.

Chocolate Strawberry Malt

Follow the recipe for the Irresistible Chocolate Malt, but add ½ cup fresh strawberries to the malt ingredients and blend. Garnish with a fresh strawberry.

Mocha Malt

Follow the recipe for the Irresistible Chocolate Malt, but add 1 teaspoon powdered instant coffee to the malt ingredients and blend. Garnish with whipped cream and a sprinkle of ground cocoa or shaved chocolate.

Through the years, Ghirardelli has published and given away many recipe packets just like these, which are early symbols of the company's on-going effort to foster a personal relationship with the cooks who use their chocolate. Most of the packets contained at least a dozen recipes, some of which were selected from the thousands submitted by loyal customers nationwide.

Chocolate-Peppermint Ice Cream Pie

YIELD: 8 SERVINGS

CRUST

1¼ cups chocolate graham cracker crumbs

4 tablespoons butter, melted

FILLING

½ cup heavy whipping cream

4 ounces (1 baking bar) Ghirardelli Bittersweet Chocolate, broken into 1-inch pieces

¼ cup firmly packed brown sugar

1 tablespoon butter

1 teaspoon pure vanilla extract

2 pints peppermint ice cream, softened

½ cup heavy whipping cream

2 tablespoons coarsely crushed striped peppermint candy

Preheat the oven to 350°. Coat a 9-inch pie pan with nonstick cooking spray.

In a large bowl, combine the chocolate graham cracker crumbs and butter, stirring until the crumbs are fully moistened. Press the mixture into the bottom and up the sides of the prepared pan. Bake 8 minutes, then cool on a wire rack. Store the cooled crust in the freezer while you prepare the filling.

In a heavy saucepan, bring the whipping cream just to a boil, then remove from the heat. Stir in the chocolate. Cover the saucepan and let it stand 5 minutes, or until the chocolate has melted. Stir the melted chocolate until smooth, then add the brown sugar, butter, and vanilla extract. Stir until the sugar has dissolved. Refrigerate 15 minutes.

Meanwhile, remove the crust from the freezer. Spoon 1 pint of the softened ice cream into the prepared crust. Spread half of the chilled sauce over the ice cream. Carefully spoon the remaining pint of the ice cream over the sauce and drizzle the remaining sauce over the top. Freeze the pie at least 2 hours, or until the ice cream is firm.

Just before serving, in small bowl, beat the whipping cream until stiff peaks form. Garnish the pie with spoonfuls of whipped cream sprinkled generously with the mint candies. Serve immediately. Store tightly covered in the freezer.

Note: Ice cream may be softened in a microwave oven on high for 10 to 15 seconds.

Baked Alaska with Chocolate Zabaglione Sauce

YIELD: 12 SERVINGS

CAKE

1 layer Chocolate Sour Cream Cake (page 30, and see note below)

1 pint (any flavor) ice cream, slightly softened

SAUCE

2 ounces (½ baking bar) Ghirardelli Semi-Sweet Chocolate, broken into 1-inch pieces

½ cup marsala wine

⅓ cup sugar

2 egg yolks, well beaten

MERINGUE

4 egg whites

1 teaspoon pure vanilla extract

¼ teaspoon cream of tartar

⅛ teaspoon salt (optional)

½ cup sugar

¼ cup sliced almonds (optional)

Prepare the Chocolate Sour Cream Cake as the recipe directs, but do not dust with confectioners' sugar. Spread the slightly softened ice cream over the top of the cooled cake to within 1 inch of the edge. Place in the freezer for several hours before you plan to serve it.

To make the sauce, melt chocolate in a double boiler over hot, but not boiling, water. Stir occasionally until the chocolate is smooth. Add the wine and sugar; stir until the sugar has dissolved. Gradually add a small amount of the chocolate mixture to the egg yolks, stirring continuously. Add the egg yolk mixture to the chocolate in the saucepan, mixing until well combined. Cook 10 minutes over low heat, or until thickened, stirring constantly. Set aside.

Preheat the oven to 450°. Transfer the cake (from the freezer) to a baking sheet and set aside. In a large bowl, beat the egg whites until foamy. Add the vanilla extract, cream of tartar, and salt. Beat on high until soft peaks form. Gradually add the sugar, beating until stiff but not dry. Spread the meringue over the ice cream, just to the edge of the cake. Sprinkle almonds over meringue. Bake 2 to 3 minutes, or until the peaks are light golden brown. Slice, drizzle with sauce, and serve immediately.

*F*licks were one of Ghirardelli's most popular products for decades, instantly identifiable in their tube-shaped red or green foil package. Flicks were shaped like coins with mounded tops, about the size of a quarter. Because their chocolate flavor came from cocoa, not chocolate liquor, they were labeled "chocolate flavored." Domingo Ghirardelli introduced flicks in the late 1800s, when each little wafer had to be hand-formed. Mercifully, it wasn't long before a machine was designed to do the job. It warmed the chocolate to the precise temperature necessary to let it drip through a tray, pierced with holes of exactly the right size, onto a moving belt. This method, called "depositing," is also used in making chocolate chips.

The popularity of the original chocolate-flavored Flicks led the company to introduce related products. Flick Instant Chocolate Flavor was marketed in the late 1950s. In this period, the company sometimes used artificial flavorings and other additives. It's not clear when this particular product faded from sight, but unlike Flicks candy, its disappearance does not seem to have brought any outcry from disappointed fans.

Ice Cream Chocolate Roll

YIELD: 10 TO 12 SERVINGS

4 eggs, separated
1 teaspoon pure vanilla extract
³⁄₄ cup Ghirardelli Sweet Ground Chocolate and Cocoa
¹⁄₄ cup boiling water
³⁄₄ cup flour
¹⁄₂ teaspoon baking powder
¹⁄₈ teaspoon salt (optional)
¹⁄₂ cup sugar
1 quart (any flavor) ice cream, softened

Preheat the oven to 325°. Grease a 15 x 10-inch jelly-roll pan, and line with waxed paper. Generously grease the waxed paper.

In a large mixing bowl, beat together the egg yolks and vanilla extract. In a separate bowl, combine ¹⁄₂ cup of the ground chocolate with the water; slowly beat into the egg mixture. In another bowl, combine the flour and baking powder. Gradually add dry ingredients to the chocolate mixture, mixing until smooth.

In a small mixing bowl, beat the egg whites with the salt until soft peaks form. Gradually add the sugar, beating until stiff but not dry. Gently fold the egg whites into the chocolate mixture. Pour batter into the prepared pan, spreading it evenly.

Bake 15 minutes, or until it springs back when lightly pressed. Run a knife around the edge of the cake. Turn out the hot cake onto a 17-inch-long piece of waxed paper. Remove the top layer of waxed paper. Starting at the narrow end, roll the cake and waxed paper jelly roll–style. Let cool.

When the cake is cool, unroll and spread it with the ice cream, forming a ¹⁄₂-inch layer. Re-roll the cake and freeze until firm. Let the cake stand at room temperature for 10 minutes before serving. Sprinkle with the remaining ¹⁄₄ cup of ground chocolate.

Peanut Butter and Chocolate Ice Cream Sandwiches

YIELD: 10 ICE CREAM SANDWICHES

½ cup butter, softened

½ cup creamy peanut butter

½ cup firmly packed brown sugar

¼ cup granulated sugar

1 egg

1 tablespoon water

1 teaspoon pure vanilla extract

1 cup flour

½ teaspoon baking powder

½ teaspoon salt (optional)

1 cup Ghirardelli Semi-Sweet Chocolate Chips

¾ cup unsalted peanuts, chopped

1½ quarts chocolate ice cream, slightly softened

Preheat the oven to 350.

In a large mixing bowl, cream the butter, peanut butter, brown sugar, and granulated sugar until well blended. Beat in the egg, water, and vanilla extract. In a separate bowl, combine the flour, baking powder and salt. Add the dry ingredients to the creamed mixture, mixing well. Stir in the chocolate chips and peanuts. For each cookie, drop 2 tablespoons of dough onto an ungreased baking sheet approximately 3 inches apart. Pat the cookies lightly until they are ¼ inch thick.

Bake 15 to 20 minutes, or until the cookies are light brown. Cool 5 minutes on the baking sheet. Transfer the cookies to a wire rack and let cool completely.

Spread ½ cup of ice cream on each of 10 cookies. Top with a second cookie and press the two halves together until the ice cream extends slightly beyond the edges of the cookies. Wrap each sandwich tightly in plastic wrap and freeze until firm, approximately 4 hours.

Ultimate Chocolate Milkshake

YIELD: TWO 10-OUNCE SHAKES

CHOCOLATE BASE

1 cup heavy whipping cream

6 ounces (1½ baking bars) Ghirardelli Semi-Sweet Chocolate, broken into 1-inch pieces

½ cup sugar

⅓ cup water

MILKSHAKE

½ cup Chocolate Base (or ⅓ cup base for less chocolaty shakes)

2 cups vanilla ice cream, softened

Sweetened Whipping Cream (page 52), for garnish (optional)

Place two 12-ounce glasses in the freezer to chill.

To make the Chocolate Base, bring the whipping cream to a boil in a heavy saucepan and immediately remove from the heat. Add the chocolate and stir. Cover the pan; let the mixture stand for approximately 5 minutes, or until melted. Stir until smooth. Add the sugar and water, stirring until the sugar has dissolved.

Combine the Chocolate Base and 1 cup of the ice cream in a blender. Blend on high until thick. Add the remaining cup of ice cream, and blend on high again until well combined. Garnish with the Sweetened Whipped Cream. Serve immediately in chilled glasses.

Strawberry-Laced Chocolate Shake

YIELD: TWO 10-OUNCE SHAKES

⅔ cup sliced fresh strawberries

⅓ cup Chocolate Base (see previous recipe)

2 cups vanilla ice cream, softened

Sweetened Whipping Cream (page 52), for garnish (optional)

Place two 12-ounce glasses in the freezer to chill.

Combine the strawberries and Chocolate Base in a blender. Blend on medium until smooth. Add 1 cup of the ice cream and blend until thick. Add the remaining cup of ice cream and blend on high again until well combined. Garnish with the Sweetened Whipped Cream. Serve immediately in chilled glasses.

Note: For another variation, substitute bananas for the strawberries in the strawberry-chocolate shake. Chocolate Base will keep for up to 1 week covered in the refrigerator. To soften ice cream, microwave on medium for 1 minute, stir, and then continue heating and stirring until spoonable.

Sauces and Toppings

Amaretto Chocolate Sauce

YIELD: ¾ CUP

¹⁄₃ cup half-and-half

*6 ounces (1¹⁄₂ baking bars) Ghirardelli Sweet Dark Chocolate,
broken into 1-inch pieces*

1 tablespoon butter, softened

2 tablespoons almond-flavored liqueur

In a heavy saucepan, bring the half-and-half to a boil and immediately remove
from the heat. Add the chocolate and stir. Cover the pan. Let stand approximately
5 minutes, or until melted. Stir the mixture until smooth. Stir in the butter until it
is melted. Stir in the liqueur until it is thoroughly incorporated. Serve warm or
when sauce has cooled to room temperature.

Store covered in the refrigerator for up to 3 days. After refrigerating, allow to
return to room temperature or place in a small microwave-safe glass bowl. Microwave
on medium for 2 to 3 minutes, stirring after 1 minute.

Pictured opposite page

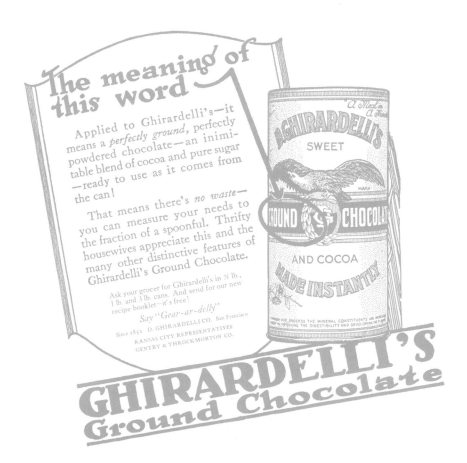

San Francisco's Victorian houses are famous for their beautiful stained-glass windows, many of which were created by the master of them all, Louis Comfort Tiffany. In the late 1970s, the craft enjoyed a revival inspiring artist Leon Richman to develop the stained-glass logo that appeared on packages of Ghirardelli chocolate into the 1980s. His designs are remarkable for accuracy as well as beauty. Less careful artists often tried to imitate stained glass by simply drawing black lines through their drawings at random. But glass can only be cut and joined together in certain, limited sections. Richman's are so true to the rules of the craft they could serve as patterns for real windows.

Chocolate–De Menthe Sauce

YIELD: 1 CUP

4 ounces (1 baking bar) Ghirardelli Semi-Sweet Chocolate, broken into 1-inch pieces

½ cup light corn syrup

¼ cup Crème de menthe

Melt the chocolate pieces in a double boiler over hot, but not boiling, water. Stir occasionally until the chocolate is smooth. Using a wire whisk, add the corn syrup and Crème de menthe until smooth. Serve warm or chilled.

To serve warm after sauce has been refrigerated, place in a small microwave-safe glass bowl. Microwave on medium for 2 to 3 minutes, stirring after 1 minute.

Easy Chocolate Sauce

YIELD: ¾ CUP

½ cup heavy whipping cream

4 ounces (1 baking bar) Ghirardelli Sweet Dark Chocolate,
broken into 1-inch pieces

Pour the whipping cream into a small microwave-safe bowl. Microwave on high for 55 to 60 seconds, or until bubbly.

Add the chocolate to the hot cream. Cover the bowl with plastic wrap and let stand 2 to 3 minutes, or until the chocolate has melted. Whisk until smooth. Serve over ice cream, pound cake, or pudding.

Ghirardelli's Hot Fudge Sauce

YIELD: 2 CUPS

4 ounces (1 baking bar) Ghirardelli Bittersweet Chocolate,
broken into ¼-inch pieces

4 tablespoons butter, cut into chunks

1½ cups sugar

½ cup water

¼ cup light corn syrup

1 teaspoon pure vanilla extract

In a heavy saucepan, combine the chocolate, butter, sugar, water, and light corn syrup. Stir the mixture continuously over medium heat until the chocolate and butter have melted and the sugar has dissolved. When the sauce comes to a boil, lower the heat and continue boiling gently for 10 minutes. Remove the thickened sauce from the heat and stir in the vanilla extract. Store covered in the refrigerator.

To reheat, place in a small microwave-safe bowl. Microwave on medium 6 to 8 minutes, stirring after the first 3 minutes.

Milk Chocolate Topping

YIELD: 2 CUPS

1½ cups evaporated milk

¾ cup sugar

2 cups Ghirardelli Milk Chocolate Chips

1 teaspoon pure vanilla extract

In a heavy saucepan, combine the milk, sugar, and chocolate chips. Whisk over medium heat until the chocolate has melted and the sugar has dissolved.

When the sauce just comes to a boil, reduce the heat to low. Cook at a low boil 5 to 8 minutes; the sauce will thicken as it cools. (If the sauce is too thick, thin it with a little milk.) Stir in the vanilla extract. Serve warm. Store tightly covered in the refrigerator for up to a week and a half.

To reheat, place in a small microwave-safe bowl. Microwave on medium 6 to 8 minutes, stirring after the first 3 minutes.

The longtime popularity of Ghirardelli baking chocolate is due to the company's special blend of cocoa beans and the unique, painstaking processing that produces a consistently rich flavor. Ghirardelli leaves all the cocoa butter in its baking chocolate for maximum richness of texture.

Hot White Fudge Sauce

YIELD: 1½ CUPS

½ cup light corn syrup

½ cup marshmallow creme

4 ounces (1 baking bar) Ghirardelli Classic White Confection, broken into 1-inch pieces

1 tablespoon butter

2 tablespoons milk

1 teaspoon pure vanilla extract

In a double boiler, combine the corn syrup, marshmallow creme, white confection, butter, and milk over hot, but not boiling, water. Stir continuously until the mixture thickens, then remove it from the heat and stir in the vanilla extract. Store tightly covered in the refrigerator for up to a week.

To reheat, place in a small microwave-safe bowl. Microwave on medium 6 to 8 minutes, stirring after the first 3 minutes.

Index

GHIRARDELLI'S COCOA

"As Pure as the roses
that glow upon the cheeks
of little children."

OVER 140 YEARS OF CHOCOLATE MAKING EXPERIENCE